SRI LA

by Frena Bloomfield

with photographs by
Tim Page and Keith MacGregor

MPC

Published by CFW Publications Ltd
1602 Alliance Building
130 Connaught Road Central
Hong Kong

Published in the UK and Europe by
Moorland Publishing Co Ltd
Moor Farm Road, Airfield Estate
Ashbourne, Derbyshire
DE6 1HD, England

Acknowledgements
I owe grateful thanks to a number of people who assisted me in the preparing and writing of this guidebook. The Ceylon Tourist Board gave me considerable guidance and assistance and made my task much easier; Amillis, my wonderful and patient driver who really introduced me to Sri Lanka; Maureen Seneviratne, that talented and scholarly writer; Bhadra Marapana, the innovator and artist of the gem industry; Roland Silva, the knowledgeable archaeologist who brought Anuradhapura alive. And then there were all the people who were just plain nice. Like Nigel and Caroline Palmer, Norman Dupont of the Galle Face Hotel, Mr White, his concierge, Samudra, who gave me the gift of her kindness. My gratitude too to Lucien Rajakarunanayake who was kind enough to read this manuscript for me, and to Kumar Pereira and Stephen Ellis for their help and encouragement.

ISBN 0 86190 209 2   Printed in Hong Kong

Masks are commonly used in sacred dance rituals of Sri Lanka

Contents

Introduction

History

From its earliest days, the island of Sri Lanka was famed for its jewels, its elephants and its spices, even when few in Europe were exactly sure just where Sri Lanka was or even what its real name was. Nevertheless, tales of its fabulous wealth trickled back through the stories told by sailors who had been there.

Sri Lanka was known to the Romans and Greeks as the island of Taprobane, a name which appears in several classical texts. Taprobane is a corruption of "Tamba-panni", an early name for Sri Lanka mentioned in the Chronicles. In the Greater Chronicle, it is explained as being derived from the world *tamba-panayo,* meaning copper-palmed. The ancient scribes say that when Vijaya, the first king of Sri Lanka, arrived from India, he and his followers fell to the ground with their hands pressed on the soil, hence copper-palmed. This seems a little unlikely. Perhaps the name was actually brought by the Tamils of India in the remembrance of a river called Tamraparni.

The Arabs called Sri Lanka *Serendib* and the Portuguese *Ceilao*. Both these names have probably come from Sinhala or Sihalam (later changed to Selan and Seren) and Dwipa (an island) changed to dib. For centuries it was known in India as Lanka (the resplendent). The Thai traders added the honorific prefix *Tewa*. The present Sri Lanka is merely the Singhalisation of Ceylon – they come from the same root.

Much of the early history of Sri Lanka is lost in the mists of mythology. Buddhists believe that the Buddha visited the island three times, but local traditions are the only record of these visits. The earliest Indian tradition says that the god Kataragama (known also as Skanda or Kartikeya, the Hindu god of war) came to the island for refuge. Again these stories are supported by local tales in certain areas of the island. The Indian epic, the *Ramayana,* relates the abduction of the Queen Sita by the King of Ceylon, Rawana, who brought her back to Ceylon. She was rescued by her husband, Rama, aided by various deities. The visitor will come across many spots linked by oral tradition to the *Ramayana* epic.

Founding of First Royal Dynasty

The first historical record which appears in the Chronicles says that Sri Lanka's first king was the Aryan Vijaya, a North Indian prince who was driven out of his own country. He and his followers arrived in Sri Lanka in about 544 BC and founded the first royal dynasty of the Singhalese.

When Vijaya arrived, the only inhabitants of Sri Lanka were three aboriginal tribes called the Rakshasas, the Yakkhas and the Nagas.

The palm-fringed beach at Bentota.

Tradition says that Vijaya's first wife was a Yakkha and that he later abandoned her for a Tamil princess from South India who became his second wife. Gradually Vijaya and his Hindu followers defeated the aboriginals, driving them further back into the forests. Because of the constant danger of new invaders from India of different tribal groups, the descendants of Vijaya retreated further inland and further up into the hills. This brought them into the Dry Zone where they constructed an impressive irrigation system.

Experts still dispute whether the art of irrigation was introduced by Vijaya or whether it already existed in Sri Lanka, but no one disputes that 2,000 years ago the inhabitants of the island of Sri Lanka boasted the most advanced water engineering of their time. In the Anuradhapura district alone there were some 11,000 small reservoirs. The Portuguese, who were the first map-makers of Sri Lanka, called them *tanque*. This has since been anglicized into "tank", an undeservedly ugly name.

Buddhism Arrives

In 307 BC, Mahinda, the son of the great Buddhist Emperor Ashoka of India, arrived in Sri Lanka and introduced Buddhism. His first convert was King Devanampiyatissa. Anuradhapura became the capital and a great center of Buddhism. But the kingdom was threatened by the Tamils of South India who launched successive invasions against the Singhalese. Finally, in AD 992, King Mahinda V abandoned Anuradhapura and retreated to the hills. There he founded the city of Polonnaruwa which flourished for three centuries until the reign of King Nissanka Malla (1187-1196) when Polonnaruwa fell. The Tamils succeeded in establishing a kingdom in the north (the area nearest to India). Singhalese kingdoms were set up in the south-west of the island and various capital cities rose and fell again. The country was laid open to other invasions from nearby neighbors in Malaya and by the Chinese, who had been trading with the Singhalese and who had greedy eyes on the riches of the island. At one point during these troubled centuries, a Chinese admiral even stole away the king of Sri Lanka to spend an unwilling couple of years in Peking, while the Chinese replaced him with a candidate of their own.

The Coming of the Colonialists

In 1505, the first of the European invaders – the Portuguese – arrived, following the spice trail. They found the weakened condition of the Sri Lankan kings much to their advantage. There were three kingdoms at the time – in Jaffna, in Kandy and at Kotte in the south-west. The Portuguese dealt with the King of Kotte and managed to get a monopoly on spices, and on cinnamon in particular. Everywhere they went, the Portuguese stole, tortured, and massacred in the name of

Christianity. Fortunately, the kingdom of Kandy was safe from the predatory Portuguese, being tucked away safely in the mountains.

The Dutch arrived in 1656 and set up friendly relations with the king of Kandy. They obligingly drove out the Portuguese before taking over as the next group of colonial masters. They were more interested in trade than in spreading their brand of Christianity, but they, too, failed to defeat the kingdom of Kandy. That was left to the British who pushed the Dutch out in 1796 and finally obtained the surrender of Kandy in 1815. Sri Lanka then became a British colony, and English its official language.

The British also set out to make a fat profit from the riches of Sri Lanka. They took over the agricultural land, built railways and established plantations. They first grew coffee, which was the major crop until a blight hit the coffee bushes.

Fortunately, the Director of the Peradeniya Botanical Gardens had foreseen that this would happen and he was ready with tea and cinchona bushes and rubber plants. Despite a common tale that the rubber plants were smuggled out of Brazil, the truth is that they were legally obtained. After the coffee blight, tea became the major crop in the hill country, rubber in the foothills and coconuts along the coastal belt. To work these plantations, the British imported cheap Tamil labor from South India. These were to become part of a serious political problem after Sri Lanka became independent in 1948.

Sri Lanka's first independent government was formed under Mr D.S. Senanayake, still regarded as the father of modern Sri Lanka.

The next few years were to see the development of the problems which still bedevil Sri Lanka today. Prices began to rise and this affected the price of rice, Sri Lanka's staple food. Considerable and often violent protests followed the spiraling prices. More problems were caused by the government's new policy of Singhalization, largely instigated by Solomon Bandaranaike and his MEP (Mahajana Eksath Peramuna) coalition. During this period Singhalese became the national language and Buddhism the national religion, which left the Hindu Tamils and the country's large Christian population in a somewhat trouble position. A considerable program of nationalization of business and foreign investments followed, which largely resulted in a downturn both in services (e.g. those of the Ceylon Transport Board) and production, (e.g. in tea and rubber plantations). However Bandaranaike was, and still is, regarded as a national hero for creating a sense of national identity. In 1959 he was assassinated by a Buddhist monk.

In the 1960s and 1970s, through numerous changes of governments and parties, Sri Lanka itself continued to suffer a downtrend in living conditions, economic prospects and supply of consumer goods. Communal violence between Singhalese and Tamils was not uncommon during this time.

The big turnabout came in 1977, when the UNP returned to power led by J.R. Jayewardene. Since then, drastic changes in financial policies have attracted foreign investment. The free trade zone is seen as a solid article of good faith to draw in more foreign investors. Rice production is high on the priority list and, with the opening of the huge Mahaveli water project, rice production is expected to increase. Most Sri Lankans are now more optimistic about taking their rightful place in the world of developing countries.

Geography and Economy

Sri Lanka is about half the size of England, measuring 445 km (276.5 miles) from north to south and 225.3 km (140 miles) across at its widest point.

Much of the island is low-lying and flat, but the south and center are hilly, extending up to the central peaks. These are very well watered and contain some spectacular waterfalls. The climate is equatorial, the main divisions being not winter and summer but monsoons. From mid-May to mid-august and again from September to November is the south-west monsoon, which brings rain to the west coast. From October to January the north-east wind which brings rain to the east coast.

Sri Lanka is geographically and climatically divided into the Wet Zone and the Dry Zone. The Wet Zone is the south-west of the island which gets rain from both monsoons, and as a result is heavily cultivated with rice, tea, rubber and fruit. The Dry Zone includes the plateaux of the north and east and extends to the mountainous areas which suffer drought during the south-west monsoon. The main product of the Dry Zone is trees, including teak, ebony and sandalwood.

About half of Sri Lanka's labor force is involved with agriculture, the main concentration being in the south-west. Much of the national income is derived from the growth and export of tea – the major export – rubber and coconuts. In recent years there have been drops in production of all three due to cost factors, world recession and climatic conditions. However, tea exports still amount to some 200 million kilos (441 million pounds) a year.

The major money-earner are chemicals, petroleum, coal, rubber and plastic products which in 1986 brought in 13.10 billion rupees from world-wide buyers.

Tourism is big business in Sri Lanka and still expanding. More than 200,000 tourists are expected by 1988 and major hotel projects are in hand now to cope with the increased numbers.

Inflation currently runs at about 30 percent per annum, because of world inflation, government expenditure on major projects and poor harvests.

(preceding page) Fishermen checking their nets at sunset, in the local outrigger canoe.

The most important development project in recent years has been the Mahaveli River Development Program. The master plan aims to provide irrigation for some 364,372 hectares (900,000 acres) to be watered by the diversion of Sri Lanka's longest river, the Mahaveli, as well as generating a great deal of hydroelectricity.

The People

There are about 15.4 million people in Sri Lanka, two-thirds of whom are Singhalese. They trace their descent from the Aryan Prince Vijaya, whose mother was said to have mated with a lion. The word "singha" – lion – is the root for the name Singhalese, which means "the lion people". The national language of Sri Lanka is now Singhalese, with Tamil coming a very poor second. The Singhalese majority live mainly in the south and, if such generalizations can be made about a while ethnic group, they are notably cheerful and easy-going in temperament. Most are Buddhists, though no longer as devout as their parents were, and they are generous and welcoming to strangers.

There is a caste system in Sri Lanka, though it is not as pronounced as in neighboring India and is often not visible at all to the casual stranger.

The Tamils are the second largest group in the country, forming about 20 percent of the population. On the whole, they are South Indian by descent and Hindu by religion. They tend to be less open in temperament and are reputed to be much more hard-working than the more leisurely Singhalese. This has increased the prosperity of the Tamils, but made them unpopular with their Singhalese compatriots.

There is increasing animosity between the Singhalese and the Tamils in a political and social sense, although it certainly should not be assumed that this exists between all Singhalese and all Tamils. The origin of this feeling goes back to British times. The British, employing their well-known "divide and conquer" technique, made much use of the disunity between the two major ethnic groups is Sri Lanka. They tended to favor the Tamils born in Sri Lanka and appointed many of them to the government and civil service. This was greatly resented by the Singhalese. The British also brought in poor Tamil labor from India to work the plantations.

After independence the Singhalese struck back. They disenfranchised the Tamil laborers who had been given citizenship, leaving them without a voice in the country of their birth and dividing them as a group from the Sri Lankan Tamils who tend to dominate trade and who have in some cases been in the country almost as long as the Singhalese themselves. The Sri Lankan Tamils, most of them living up in Jaffna and in the north and east of the country, feel that they have increasingly been cut out of decision-making at high political levels. In recent years this has led to the formation of the Tamil United Liberation Front, which is pushing hard for political power and even for the formation of a separate Tamil state. Meanwhile, the government is running a repatriation scheme for tea-plantation Tamils to send them back to India.

In addition to the Indian Tamils laboring on the tea estates, there are a number of other small ethnic communities of Indian origin – the Parsees, Borahs, Sindhis, Memons, Nadars, Bharathas, Gujeratis, Chetties and Malayalees.

An important minority in Sri Lanka are the Muslims, often called the Moors. They are either descendants of the Arab traders who settled in Sri Lanka from the 11th century onwards or Muslim immigrants from India. There are about 900,000 of them.

Another community with a high profile is that of the Burghers. Although a number of people call themselves Burghers, those who are entitled to do so are the Eurasians descended from the Dutch and other Europeans who served under the Dutch East India Company. Unlike the Anglo-Indians of India, the Burghers of Sri Lanka have always been, and still are, highly regarded. They were favored by their colonial masters and even under independence they still retain much of their status. This is perhaps largely because those who married the European traders came from high-status Singhalese families.

They are a few old colonials left on the island. They can sometimes be found up in the hills, especially around Nuwara Eliya. There are also a very small number of hardy businessmen who did not hotfoot it back home to Europe, but who stayed to invest their courage and efforts in the new Sri Lanka. Sri Lanka's most famous foreigner is probably Arthur C. Clarke, the science fiction writer, who has made the country his home for the past twenty years.

Religion

The national religion of Sri Lanka is Buddhism and is largely followed by the Singhalese. It is the southern school of Buddhism which dominates the island, the Theravada or Hinayana (Lesser Vehicle) school. In this philosophy, the followers try to work for their own salvation.

The central beliefs of all schools of Buddhism are that life is suffering and illusion and that man can only be freed from the endless cycle of suffering and rebirth by meditation and religious observance.

Buddhism was introduced to Sri Lanka by Mahinda, the monk son of the emperor Ashoka who converted the Singhalese king in about 247 BC thereby changing the whole history of the island. Since then it has been Buddhism which has served to unify the population – in social organization, custom, art and architecture.

Theravada Buddhist monks, who are to be seen almost everywhere.

Although the practice of Buddhism in Sri Lanka is less pure than it was before, the devout are still to be found. Many monks, learned in the ways of traditional medicine, run free or nearly free clinics for the sick.

One feature of Buddhist temples throughout Sri Lanka that may puzzle visitors is the fact that the statues of Hindu deities, such as Vishnu, Kataragama or Pattini, can be found within. This is usually explained as being a gesture of politeness to the Hindu wives of some of the early Singhalese kings. To keep these royal spouses happy, a familiar deity was included in a Buddhist shrine. More accurately, it may simply be a slight corruption of pure Theravada Buddhism which arises from the nearness of India and indeed the presence of a large Hindu population.

The Tamils are Hindus and their temples (*kovils*) are brightly colored with a three-dimensional pantheon of figures round the entrance and often as a complete frieze round the walls.

Christianity has its following too, especially among the Burghers, but also among other groups. The Roman Catholic Church numbers fishing communities among its faithful; around the village of Negombo the whole area is known as Little Rome for its keen Catholicism. In fact a special Easter Passion Play is presented there every year by the fisherfolk. And two islands in the north – Kachchativu and Palativu – see major pilgrimages each February and March to the churches of Saint Anthony.

General Information

When to go

Sri Lanka has a fairly equable climate and much depends upon the visitor's intended destinations within the country. The west and southern parts of the island are cold and rainy from about April to June and again from September to November. The east of the island, or the hills, is often rainy from October to January. The delightful thing is that there is always one half of the island with good weather. The high season is from October to January, when tourists arrive to enjoy the south coast sunshine. Prices too are high at this time. If sunshine and peace is what you need, consider trying the east coast from April onwards.

Climate

The two monsoon seasons in Sri Lanka tend to complicate timings for visits. Being tropical, temperatures tend to be warm through to hot. Temperatures in Colombo, for example, range from 27°C (80°F) to a high of 35°C (95°F) between March and June. The coolest time is from November to January. In the hills, temperatures are lower. When Colombo is 27°C (80°F), Kandy is likely to be 20°C (68°F), while Nuwara Eliya dips to 16°C (61°F). Whenever you go to the hills, take warm clothing. A sweater and, in the rainy season, a whole winter wardrobe will not come amiss. It can feel very cold, especially after the warmth of the plains.

The south-west monsoon brings rain to the south and west side of the island from April to June, and again from September to November. The north-east hits the east coast from October to January. However, during the time between the two monsoons there can be heavy thunderstorms throughout the whole island.

Festivals

Most of the festivals of Sri Lanka are religious and a few are political. The birthdays of the Buddha, Christ and Mohammed are all public holidays, as are the full moon days of every month. These Buddhist holidays are known as *puja*. Many of the festivals occur on the lunar calendar and are therefore not fixed at the same time each year on the Gregorian calendar. For finalized dates of festivals, check with a Sri Lankan Embassy or Consulate or, in the case of a big festival, with a travel agent.

There are a number of regularly occurring big festivals:

January: The **Duruthu Perahera** is held at the Kelaniya Temple outside Colombo on the full moon day, to celebrate the Buddha's legendary visit to the site.

On January 14th, the **Thai Pongal** harvest festival is celebrated by Hindus in honor of the Sun God.

February: **Independence Day** falls on the 4th, with parades and processions all over the country.

In late February or early March comes the Hindu Festival commemorating the marriage of Siva and Parvati.

Up in the Jaffna peninsula, the islands of Kachchaitivu and Palaitivu become pilgrimage centers for Roman Catholics who visit the churches dedicated to Saint Anthony.

March: An **Easter Passion Play** is performed by the fishing people of Duwa, near Negombo.

April: Both the **Singhalese** and the **Tamil New Year Festivals** fall around this time. This is also the start of the south-west monsoon and the end of the season for climbing Adam's Peak (see p.103).

May: May the First is **Workers' Day** and the 22nd is **Republic Day,** but the big holiday of May is **Wesak**, the full moon celebration of the anniversary of the Buddha's birth, enlightenment and death. Village festivities are to be found everywhere, with visits to the temples, offerings of flowers and the lighting of lamps throughout the island.

June: **Poson**, on the full moon day, marks the coming of Mahinda to Sri Lanka, bearing the teachings of the Buddha. Most pilgrims go the the sacred city of Anuradhapura for this and also visit the nearby shrine of Mihintale.

July/August: This is the time of the most colorful festival of the year, and one of the greatest spectacles in Asia – the **Kandy Asala Perahera**. It continues for ten days and nights and features glorious parades of elephants, dancers, drummers and officiating priests.

In July, the pilgrimage from Batticoloa to Kataragama starts. While the Kandy Perhera is on, so too is the Hindu festival of Vel in Colombo. The golden chariot of the Hindu god of war, Kataragama, is dragged like a Juggernaut from the Hindu temple in Sea Street to the kovil at Bambalapitiya. At the sacred Hindu shrine at Kataragama itself the whole gamut of Hindu worship and spectacle can be seen – processions, offerings, fire-walking and self-torture of various kinds.

September: The 26th is **Bandaranaike Commemoration Day.**

October/November: The loveliest of all Hindu festivals, **Deepavali,** (the Festival of Lights) comes at this time, after the harvest. It is marked by

(above) A religious procession – or perahera – on the road to Badulla.
(opposite page) One of the magnificently caparisoned elephants taking part in the Kandy Asala Perahera.

the lighting of oil lamps and candles to welcome back Lakshmi, the goddess of wealth.

December: The pilgrimage season to **Adam's Peak** begins. The full moon day commemorates the Princess Sangamitta, the daughter of the emperor Ashoka, who came to Sri Lanka with her brother Mahinda and who brought with her a sapling from the original Bo tree under which the Buddha found enlightenment.

Visas

Citizens of Great Britain, Ireland, Malaysia, Pakistan, Singapore, Australia, Japan, New Zealand, Philippines, Thailand, Canada, USA and most European countries do not require entry visas and can stay for up to thirty days.

Nationals of most other countries need visas prior to arrival in Sri Lanka. Any Sri Lankan Embassy or Consulate or, failing that, British Embassy can advise.

To extend your visa, go to the Department of Immigration and Emigration, Galle Buck, Colombo 1, Unit 06, tel: 29851/21509. You will be required to produce a valid passport, an onward ticket and evidence of sufficient funds.

Stay Permits

On arrival, a stay permit of one month is usually given. For extensions, go to the Immigration Department.

Be warned! The Immigration Department is permanently surrounded by an enormous mob of people fighting to get into the one small door which is the entrance to the entire Department. Visitors wishing to stay beyond one month are also required to report to the Aliens Bureau, 4th floor, New Secretariat Building, Colombo 1 to register themselves as aliens.

Customs

Arrival: Visitors are required to fill in a customs cum immigration card which must then be produced every time money is changed in Sri Lanka. This will also be needed at the time of departure from Sri Lanka and will enable the visitor to change remaining Sri Lankan money for other currencies.

Declare all currencies on arrival, as well as articles of high value, Sri Lankan gems set or unset, firearms and dangerous weapons, and commercial quantities of any goods. The customs officers are usually interested in electronics too.

Visitors are allowed to bring in one and a half liters of spirits, two regular size bottles of wine; perfume for personal use; and 200 cigarettes or 50 cigars. They are not allowed to import more than 250 rupees in Indian, Pakistani or Sri Lankan currencies.

Departure: There is an embarkation tax for those leaving Sri Lanka. At the moment it is Rs.200 for those leaving by air, and Rs.5 for those leaving by sea. (These taxes are subject to change.)

Visitors wishing to convert Sri Lankan currency must produce their currency forms, providing that they exchanged the money in the first place.

Tourists may take out any permitted articles bought in Sri Lanka, provided that they are not in commercial quantities. Gems may be exported tax free, provided they were bought with imported currency as declared on the landing card.

No antiques or products made from any part of a protected species can be exported. They will be confiscated at the airport.

There are Duty Free Shops in the airport where a full range of imported goods can be bought with foreign currency.

Attention! You can only spend foreign currency once you have passed through into the Departure Lounge, even if you only want a cup of coffee.

On Arrival at Colombo Airport

Passengers arriving at Colombo Airport can buy duty-free goods at the duty-free counter which is situated before the health and immigration checkpoints.

A customs declaration form must be signed, checked by the customs official, then retained by the passenger throughout his visit. When departing, the form will be collected again by the customs officials. Visitors are required to re-export articles brought in as personal effects. Cameras, radios, recorders and sound equipment declared on arrival must be taken out of the country again.

After clearing customs and immigration, passengers wishing to go into Colombo would be well advised to take a taxi – even though these are expensive. The journey will cost well over a hundred rupees, but there is no satisfactory bus service from the airport into the city. If you are staying at a major hotel, arrange for a hotel car to meet you at the airport. It will be worth the extra expense. Don't ride in a taxi unless it is properly registered and is fitted with a meter.

Tourist Information

If you want general tourist information, there is a Tourist Information Centre in the airport which is open any day during arrivals and departures.

For information on what to see and where to go in Sri Lanka, visit the Tourist Information Centre (TIC) at 321, Galle Road, Colombo 3, tel: 573175 and at Transworks House, Ministry of State, Colombo 1. They have a number of useful leaflets to give away, as well as tourist maps in English, French, German and Italian. This office is open from Monday to Friday, 8.30 am until 4.45 pm and on weekends and public holidays from 8am until 12.30 pm. The staff are friendly and helpful.

For those heading for Kandy, there is a Tourist Information Centre at Kandyan Arts Association Building, 72, Victoria Drive, Kandy. Open Monday to Friday from 8 am to 6 pm and on weekends and public holidays from 8 am to 4 pm.

Guides

The Tourist Information Centres can arrange and registered guides for you. They are identified by a special card issued by the Ceylon Tourist Board. You can also get them through the Travel Information Centre, tel: 589585-6 or the Approved Travel Guide Lecturers Association, tel: 598346 between 9 am to 4 pm and 713675 at other times.

This will cost Rs.225 a day for English speaking guide, and an additional fee of Rs.25 per day in any other foreign language. However, even the registered guides sometimes do not seem to be properly equipped with information, and you may find the service somewhat disappointing.

If you are hiring a car with a driver, you do not need a guide as well. Your driver will speak English quite well enough to meet your needs. Do not be persuaded to take a guide as well. You will merely be doubling your expenses.

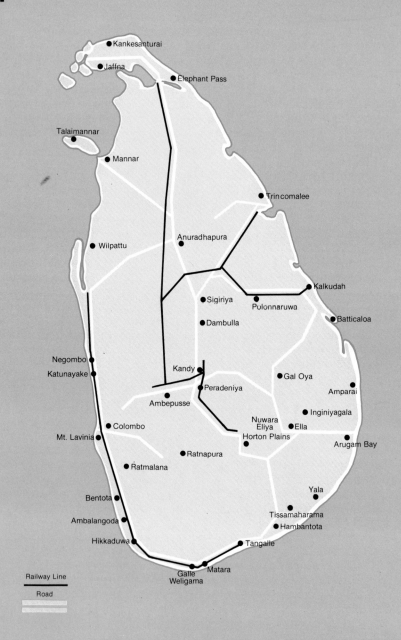

SRI LANKA

N

Kankesanturai
Jaffna
Elephant Pass
Talaimannar
Mannar
Trincomalee
Wilpattu
Anuradhapura
Kalkudah
Sigiriya
Polonnaruwa
Batticaloa
Dambulla
Negombo
Kandy
Gal Oya
Katunayake
Peradeniya
Amparai
Ambepusse
Inginiyagala
Colombo
Nuwara Eliya
Ella
Mt. Lavinia
Horton Plains
Arugam Bay
Ratnapura
Ratmalana
Yala
Bentota
Tissamaharama
Ambalangoda
Hambantota
Hikkaduwa
Tangalle
Galle
Matara
Weligama

Railway Line

Road

yiu

Many sites of interest have local guides available. If they are government department workers – such as you will find on many archaeological sites – use them to guide you round and give them a reasonable tip afterwards. If they are apparently just acting as touts, ignore them. They may tell a pretty tale, but they probably do not know what they are talking about.

Maps

Large scale maps of the island are available at the Survey Department, Map Sales Branch, Kirula Road, Narahenpita, tel: 585111/585112-6 and Map Sales Centre, York Street, Colombo 1, tel: 35328. Do not buy them from inside your hotel or from a street tout, as you will be overcharged. Buy them from a department store, a bookstore or a general store.

If you are driving or being driven in Sri Lanka, you will need a good map in order to take the more interesting side roads.

Tourist Police

Like many other tourism-conscious countries, Sri Lanka has its own Tourist Police. If you have any problems which need police intervention or help – overcharging by taxi drivers, stolen property – the office is on the ground floor, New Secretariat Building. Colombo 1, Fort, tel: 26941/21111. There are other Tourist Police branch offices at Mount Lavinia, Negombo and the National Holiday Resort at Bentota. They are said to be very good at getting back lost property.

Photography Permits

If you want to take pictures of Sri Lanka's prime archaeological sites, you will have to pay for the privilege. This is not as unreasonable as you may at first think. This is a developing country which needs all the foreign exchange it can get. Most of the money taken from photographic permits and entrance fees to sites goes towards keeping those same sites in a good state of preservation.

Tickets are issued at the Cultural Triangle Office (Ministry of Cultural Affairs), Malay Street, Colombo 2, tel: 587912. These tickets provide admission to and permission to photograph all Cultural Triangle archaeological sites, monuments and museums. A round trip visit and picture permit costs Rs.330.

Individually, the sites cost the following:

Anuradhapura, Polonnaruwa and Sigiriya Rs.110; Dambulla, Kandy and Nalanda Rs.82.50. Tickets can be bought from 8.30 am to 4.15 pm on weekdays only.

Sri Lankans do not have to pay to enter sites. This is just a way of allowing Sri Lankans to see their own heritage, while visitors who can well afford it pay to keep up these sites.

Health

Regulations: If you have visited a smallpox-infected country in the 14 days before entering Sri Lanka, a vaccination certificate against smallpox will be required.

Immunization against cholera is not required, though it might be a wise precaution.

Visitors arriving from areas infected with yellow fever should have valid certificates of vaccination against yellow fever.

Hospitals: Most foreign visitors are not enthusiastic about the state of Sri Lanka's public hospitals, but it is reassuring to know that in an emergency they are there and they offer a comprehensive service.

In Colombo, the Colombo General Hospital has an out-patient department at Regent Street, Colombo 8, tel: 91111.

For expectant mothers there is the Castle Street Maternity Hospital, tel: 596231 or the De Soysa Maternity Hospital, tel: 596224.

For emergencies involving the eyes, there is the New Eye Hospital, tel: 593911.

For those with children in need of pediatric care, there is the Lady Ridgeway Children's Hospital, tel: 593711.

Sri Lanka also has a highly-developed natural medical system, known as ayurvedic medicine, and there is a Government Ayurvedic Hospital at Cotta Road, Borella, tel: 595855-6.

There are also many private doctors and hospitals and most hotels can help you to contact them. The big hotels have resident doctors.

Chemists: Most chemists and drug stores dispense drugs and act as pharmacists. Many drugs can be bought over the counter. Chemist shops are numerous in Colombo and most provincial towns.

Drinking Water: It is advisable to drink only water that has been boiled and filtered. Most hotels offer filtered water as well as a range of aerated waters. If you are in doubt about the water, do not drink it. Instead, drink hot tea or a bottled drink. Also avoid drinks with ice cubes in them, as the ice cubes are unlikely to have been made from boiled filtered water. If you want a good safe thirst-quencher, drink coconut juice which is cheap and delicious.

Money

The Sri Lankan unit of currency is the *rupee* (Rs.) divided into 100 cents. There are rupee notes in denominations of 2, 5, 10, 50, 100, 500 and 1,000 while the coins are 1c, 2c, 5c, 10c, 25c, 50c, one rupee and five rupees. When you change your money on arriving at the airport, you will be given as much as possible in 100-rupee notes. Break these down as soon as you can and keep a good handful of Rs.2 notes. Rs.100 is a lot of money to the average Sri Lankan and few people will be able to give you change. These two-rupee notes will be very useful for tipping.

If you intend to take public buses, you will need small change in coins, which tends to be rare in Sri Lanka. As in other Asian countries, people are often reluctant to give you your full change in small coins. They are not really cheating you. They know five or ten cents is irrelevant to you, while they will need it to give to other Sri Lankan shoppers.

Avoid taking dirty, worn or torn notes from anyone. You will be landed with them, as many people refuse to accept them as currency. This is also true of the foreign currency you take into Sri Lanka. It should be in almost perfect condition or you will be unable to change it.

For some reason you always get slightly more for your travelers' cheques than for your cash currency which reverses the usual trend. You also get better value in a bank than in a hotel.

There is virtually no black market in money in Sri Lanka, so do not waste time and energy looking for it. Beware if anyone offers you a high rate of exchange – you may be in danger of being set up for a robbery.

When you arrive in Sri Lanka you will be given a currency form. Keep it. You will need it to change money at the beginning and the end of your trip.

As a very rough guide, the rate of exchange is:

Australian dollar	22.70 Sri Lankan rupees
American dollar	30.87
Pound sterling	58.25

Foreign currencies other than pounds sterling, American dollars, German deutschmarks and Japanese yen are not necessarily accepted at provincial banks and you should change enough money for your needs before leaving Colombo.

Banking hours run between 9 am to 1 pm on Monday and from 9 am to 1.30 pm on other weekdays. Banks are closed on Saturdays, Sundays and public holidays. Most international banks are represented in Colombo. There is an all-night bank at the Inter-Continental Hotel and in Fort district next to the Gem Corporation. Both are branches of the Bank of Ceylon and are also open on Sundays and public holidays.

Tipping

Tipping is optional, but you will of course get better service if you are known as a good tipper. Many hotels and restaurants now include a 10 percent service charge as part of their bill. In such cases the staff do in fact get a generous share of that at the end of the month. If you want to tip your room staff in the hotel, give to each one individually and privately. Otherwise you will have a long queue of people whom you have never even seen before lining up in front of you. If you want good room service, leave an extra rupee or two on the tray each time you order.

Where no service charge is included, you should leave about 10 per cent extra for the staff.

A site guide will be hoping for a tip from you, even if he is a government servant. Two rupees will make him happy, five delighted and 10 ecstatic. The same goes for people who give you personal service of some kind.

As for your driver, that is a difficult question. You are already paying for his services, plus he will be getting a commission of anything from eight percent up to 45 percent on almost everything along the way – your hotel room, your meals, your souvenir purchases. Therefore you may not want to add on the suggested 50 rupees a day extra that the TIC suggests as a final tip.

The same goes for your guide, if you have one. He and the driver will be splitting the commission. So it is up to you to decide what you wish to afford on top of the hire fees. A generous tip will be expected, however.

Traveling Inside Sri Lanka

If you want to see a reasonable range of Sri Lanka's attractions, you really should stay for at least seven days and ideally for longer. It is, fortunately, a country quite well served by transport and small enough to allow the visitor to see different areas within a short period of time. It only takes a day to travel the entire length of the island by train, from Colombo to Jaffna.

Sri Lanka is also blessed with a prodigality of beautiful scenery, and it is almost impossible to find a road that is dull or ugly. As there is a fairly well developed road system, the sightseer can make rapid progress from one region to the other. Progress should not be too rapid, however, as many of the real delights of Sri Lanka are those casual roadside sights.

Transport

The whole country is linked by the public bus system of the Ceylon Transport Board. Rates, says the Board's publicity, are the cheapest in the world, and there is a lesson to be learned from that. Private minibuses, which most Sri Lankans tend to use, run along the same routes. There is the train, which links certain areas of the country together. There is also a domestic air service between major areas and a helicopter service for a more limited range. The best choice is a hire car, whether self-drive or with the driver.

Self-Drive

Several major international car-hire firms are represented in Colombo. Hertz, American International and Inter-Rent are represented by Quickshaws Ltd., Kalinga Place, Colombo 5 (Hertz, tel: 83133). Avis is represented by Mack Transport Ltd., Mackinnons Building, 11A, York Street, Colombo 1, tel: 29881-9.

A dancer from the Kandy Asala Perhera.

Cars are very expensive (and so is petrol) in Sri Lanka which is why you see so many old cars. One journalist described Colombo as the place where Morris Minors go to die. This obviously makes car hire fairly expensive. The rates for non air-conditioned car range from Rs.280 to Rs.400 and air-conditioned from Rs.500 to Rs.600 per day up to a minimum of 80 km (50 miles) or 100 km (62 miles). for excess mileage from Rs.4 to Rs.4.50 per running kilometer.

Car Hire

To hire a car with a driver costs anything from Rs.6 per kilometer (0.62 mile) upwards, plus a driver's daily allowance which is about Rs.50 per day at the time of writing.

If you do hire a car and driver, you will pay through the nose if you hire one from your hotel. Instead, ask around for a recommended driver. If you decide to hire a driver who touts your custom, make sure he turns up in the vehicle agreed upon. It is not unknown for drivers to contract for one handsome vehicle and turn up in an old wreck. Sri Lankan roads can be bumpy, so you do need a car with good springs. Do not pay your driver in advance, though he may need petrol money in advance from time to time.

Bus

Few Sri Lankans have a good word to say for the Ceylon Transport Board. Which is sad, as everyone thought it was a good idea when in a burst of socialism the government decided to abolish private ownership of transport firms and nationalize the lot into one big happy family to the great advantage of the citizens. Of course it did not turn out that way. Instead the huge Ceylon Transport Board has lumbered itself almost to a standstill. Buses are overcrowded, slow and much in need of renovation. They are cheap, it is true, but so tortuous that most Sri Lankans avoid them whenever possible. The official line on buses is that there are special express services to principal towns on which seats may be booked in advance (tel: 28081, the Central Bus Station, Olcott, Mawatha, Colombo 11).

However, most citizens of Sri Lanka would suggest you go to the central terminus and pick up one of those smart-looking private minibuses which ply between one town and another. They cost a little more, but not much, and they only take as many passengers as there are seats, so you will be comfortable.

Rail

Most visitors enjoy a little train travel. Trains are reasonably comfortable and not very crowded and they give you ample opportunity to enjoy the countryside, as well as getting to meet a number of people who live in Sri Lanka.

The trains are operated by the Sri Lanka Government Railway and they run regularly from Colombo to all the most important tourist sites – Kandy, Anuradhapura, Polonnaruwa, Galle, Hikkaduwa, Bentota, Matara, Nanu-Oya (the spectacular run up to Nuwara Eliya), Jaffna, Batticoloa, Trincomalee, Negombo, Bandarawela, Haputale, Diyatalawa and Talawakelle.

All long distance trains have second- and third-class accommodation and there is first-class accommodation in trains with sleeping berths. some of the most scenic routes have observation cars – especially those that travel in the hills – for which you can reserve seats. You can buy a ticket not more than ten days before your journey and it is in fact easy to buy last-minute tickets for most trains.

For tickets and reservations, go to Colombo Fort Railway Station any weekday from 8.30 am to 3.30 pm, and between 8.30 am and noon on Sundays. For telephone information, call 21281 extension 356, the Booking Office, the Colombo Fort Railway.

It is also possible to take a special railway tour, such as a one-day trip to Kandy, Hikkaduwa or Polonnaruwa, in air-conditioned cars with lunch provided. The fees included services of a guide. For details, call 35838.

Ferry

There used to be a ferry boat service to South India which operated out of Talaimannar to carry both passengers and vehicles. The service is temporarily suspended. For details, contact the Tourist Information Centre at 321 Galle Road, Colombo 3, tel: 573175.

Taxis

Taxis are available in most towns in Sri Lanka, and can usually be spotted by their yellow tops and red numbers on white licence plates. They are expensive, mainly because petrol is expensive. The minimum rate per 1.6 km (one mile), at the time of writing, is Rs.8. Make sure that the driver puts the flag down on the meter. If he does not, call the police or at least get out of the cab, because you will certainly be overcharged. For complaints, call the Tourist Police, tel: 26941, but make sure you have the vehicle number.

Communications

Telephone and Cable Facilities

International telegraph, telex and telephone services are available at the Central Telegraph Office, Duke Street, Colombo 1, tel: 27176. Some of these services are also offered by the major hotels.

Unless absolutely necessary, you should get all such business done while you are Colombo. These services are frequently reliable elsewhere.

It is almost impossible to get telephone connections from other parts of the country. There are supposed to be direct telephone services by satellite 24 hours a day to the United Kingdom, Australia, Singapore, Malaysia, Hong Kong, Italy, China, Japan and India, and there are links to most other parts of the world; in reality it can take up to several hours to place an overseas call from other parts of the country, if you can place it at all.

This said, it is an irony that it can be quicker to call overseas than to obtain a Sri Lankan number. Many of the country's main towns are directly linked by a dialing service, although this may not work either. Towns not linked by trunk dialing have to be reached by booked calls.

Mail

Visitors sometimes complain that their holiday mail does not always arrive from Sri Lanka, but in general it seems to be reasonably dependable. The latest postal rates can be obtained from the General Post Office, Janadhipathi Mawatha, Colombo 1, where there is also a Poste Restante service.

The Media

There are a number of daily newspapers published in Sri Lanka, in English, Sinhala and Tamil. Virtually all newspapers are government-owned or controlled, which limits their coverage. The weekend supplements tend to be the most interesting for visitors as they often carry cultural and historical background features. There is a small range of foreign newspapers and magazines around, in hotels, bookstalls and newsagents, but they are expensive.

Television starts at 6 pm and closes down by 11 pm. There is a color service and programs range from early programs for children through to news and general entertainment. A number of foreign series can be seen.

Radio services run from 5.30 am until 11pm and there are transmissions in six languages – Sinhala, Tamil, English, Hindi, Urdu and Arabic. This also includes commercial broadcasts.

Shopping

There is quite a wide variety of things to buy in Sri Lanka but a number of visitors express disappointment that creative standards are not higher. Nevertheless, if you keep you eyes open as you travel around the country, you often find things of great charm, handicrafts of a high standard and for more modest prices than you will find in the cities. When you see something you like, buy it! Goods are often produced very regionally in Sri Lanka and you may never see them again once you have passed them by.

(preceding page) South-west coastal surf breaking on the beach.

Batik: This tends to be overrated, overproduced and overpriced in Sri Lanka, which is a pity since batik can be quite an art form. You will find batik clothing, household draperies and purely decorative paintings. Bargain hard when you find something you like.

Silver: Most silver in Sri Lanka is known as Kandyan silver and it is not very pure. It is a silver and alloy mix and a great deal of jewelry is made of this. You can also find trays, ornaments and tea and coffee sets in silver.

Brass: If you like brass, you should enjoy Sri Lanka. There is a lot of brass handiwork being done, though much of it is very thin stuff indeed with stereotyped designs. Every Sri Lankan household usually has its special brassware, so ask a Sri Lankan where you can get the good stuff. Be prepared to pay well, though.

Ceramics: There are some very good ceramics being made in Sri Lanka now – from big chunky things to delicate porcelain – and it seems to be one of the real bargains available.

Trinketry: There are a lot of small things made from various materials – carved bone, tortoise shell, lacquerwork, quillwork, ebony and ivory. Many countries do not allow you to import these materials, though, and products made from protected species cannot be exported out of Sri Lanka.

Masks: Many tourists buy the brightly painted masks of Sri Lanka which are on sale everywhere.

Rattan, bamboo and rushware: This is used by the women of Sri Lanka, but goods made from these materials make splendid souvenirs. Look around the local markets for these and be prepared to bargain.

Gems: It is highly unlikely that you will wish to leave Sri Lanka without buying its most famous product, a gemstone. The extensive variety of gemstones to be found includes:

Corundun – blue sapphires, star sapphires (these contain 'silk' or tiny occlusions which give the star effect), rubies and yellow, pink, orange and white sapphires. This group of stones is the hardest.
Chrysoberyl – cat's eye, chrysoberyl, alexandrite. In recent years alexandrite has become very popular, especially with the Japanese. It is prized for its color changes: green in natural light, changing to red under artificial light. The stone is found only in Sri Lanka and Russia, but the largest sizes occur in Sri Lanka. The British Museum has two fine specimens from the island, weighing 43 and 27.5 carats respectively.
Spinel – blue, red and purple spinel.
Topaz – white and blue, which is very rare.
Zircon – green, yellow and brown. In Matara, the white zircon is known as the Matara diamond, so do not get too excited if you are offered a very cheap diamond there.

Garnet – pyrope, almondine and hessonite.
Beryl – aquamarine. The emerald is the most famous member of this family, but it is not found in Sri Lanka.
Chalcedony – agate.
Quartz – smoky, white, citrine, amethyst, quartz cat's eye. The colors range from purple to almost black.
Tourmaline – brown.
Feldspar – moonstone. This is really Sri Lanka's national stone. It is smooth and milky grey in color, while the best have a certain bluish sheen to them. It is very cheap to buy.

There are also some other rare gems which you are unlikely to be offered. These include sinhalite, konerupine, iodolite, indicolite and andalusite fibrolite.

Sri Lanka: Famous for its Gems

The name Sri Lanka is synonymous with gems and this has been true ever since it was first known to the outside world. Early Romans knew Taprobane, as they called Sri Lanka, for its gems and its pearls. Sailors returning to Arabia from the island they called Serendib were full of stories of precious jewels and riches, which became incorporated into the Tales of the Arabian Nights and the adventures of Sinbad the legendary sailor. Mythology says that it was to Tarshish – or Sri Lanka – that the Biblical King Solomon sent for the jewels that helped him win the heart of the Queen of Sheba.

The Gem Industry

The traditional center of the gem industry is Ratnapura, the "city of gems". As a city, Ratnapura is undistinguished. But it is here that the gem trade was founded, probably because it is at the geographical center of the area where gems are most commonly found.

The most actively gemmed areas are around the town itself, and Eheliyagoda, Kuruwita, Pelmadulla, Kalawana and Rakwana. Small extensions of the gem areas are to be found in certain western and southern provinces and gems are additionally often found in rivers. The likeliest of these are the Getahetta Oya, near Eheliyagoda, the Denawaka Ganga between Pelmadulla and Ratnapura, the Weganga between Kahawatta and Ratnapura, and the Hangamuwa and Niriella Gangas.

Most mines are fairly small and work on a co-operative basis. The owner of the land gets a cut, so does the foreman, while the daily laborers get a small wage, their food and a share of the profits from stones found.

There are many small mines like this around Ratnapura. They look like wooden tents in the middle of a field, built over a hole. All such

Mining gems in Ratnapura.

mines are subject to government control and licence, which is why mining is also done illegally in depths of the forests and national parks, away from prying eyes.

Usually laborers are quite happy to show you what they are doing and may also try to sell a few stones. Buy them if they are cheap, but otherwise refuse and make do with donating a small tip for their time instead.

Gem-Cutting

Unless they are of exceptional size, gemstones have to be cut to have any real value. The whole process of cutting and preparing gems can be seen in Ratnapura at the Ratnapura Gem Bureau, in Getangama, Ratnapura. The Gem Bureau is privately owned and it is run by Bhadra Marapone, the golden boy of the modern gem industry.

Basically, these methods have not changed in centuries. Back in the early days of history, gems were never cut. They were merely bored through the center with a big hole and strung round the wearer's neck – a method crude enough to reduce the whole of Hatton Garden to tears. Things are somewhat more advanced now.

Today, the stones are cut on a revolving disc made of lead reinforced with an abrasive powder of silicon carbide. The cutting disc is mounted on a shaft driven by a hand-operated bow string and the cutter holds the stone against the cutting edge. This rounds off the stone. After this, they are polished by a similar method, but the disc this time is made of copper or brass. The actual polishing is done with rouge or a paste made of the ash from burnt paddy husks.

The first gem-cutters were the Moors and even today the industry is dominated by them. No Singhalese official likes to talk about this though, as it is something of a sore point.

Sri Lanka has been the source of some of the world's most famous gems, including the so-called Star of India. It is a huge star sapphire, straight out of the Sri Lankan gem-bearing gravel. It got its name after being taken to India for expert cutting and now resides in the Museum of Natural History in New York, still under its spurious title. Another Sri Lankan treasure was the 466-carat Blue Sapphire, which has disappeared discreetly into an American private collection. The Blue Giant of the Orient, a sapphire weighing in at 500 carats, and the 400-carat Blue Belle of Asia both came from Sri Lanka.

Where to Buy Gems

You might as well admit from the start that, as a visitor to Sri Lanka – unless you are already a gem dealer – it is unlikely that you know enough about gems to best some of the villains you will find trying to sell their wares. Do not buy tempting little stones allegedly just found by a field worker, unless you pay so little that it does not matter. Your chances of finding a bargain are slight.

The best places to buy gems are either at the government-run State Gem Corporation or the Ratnapura Gem Bureau. Do not buy jewels being sold from the boot of a Mercedes parked by the road. Do not even buy at your hotel's shopping mall, as it will be overpriced.

There are several Gem Corporation branches in Colombo, selling unset and set gems. Their settings tend to be a bit fifties flamboyant, but they can also set your own designs and do a very good job.

The main showroom is at Macan Markar Building, 24 York Street, Colombo 1, tel: 23377, 23075, 28701.

Where to Stay in Ratnapura

By far the best choice is the interesting Hotel Kalawathie in Polhengoda Village, about 1.6 km (one mile) outside Ratnapura. It is well designed, with many original works of art and handicraft used as decoration, and it is surrounded by what will be a three-acre herb garden, now in its first stages but eventually to be a complete living catalogue of medicinal and food herbs. The rooms are excellent in design and maintenance, the Sri Lankan food delicious, European less so.

It is good for peace and quiet, and is near the Sinharajah Rain Forest, the Uda Walawe National Park and an impressive array of temples, waterfalls and tea plantations. Not cheap but certainly reasonable.

Recreation

Cinema: Colombo has a number of air-conditioned cinemas which show a variety of British, American, Continental, East European and Singhalese films. These are listed in the daily papers. They are more heavily censored than in Western countries and you may have to buy tickets ahead of the performance in the case of very popular films. Check with your hotel.

Theater: There are frequent stagings of Western, Singhalese and translated plays in Colombo. The best known theaters are the Lionel Wendt Theatre (Guildford Crescent, Colombo 7), the Lumbini Theatre (Havelock Town, Colombo 5), and the Tower Hall (Maradana, Colombo 10).

Nightclubs: Most of the big hotels have nightclubs which provide dinner, dancing and sometimes a floorshow. It is unlikely that it will be up to international standards in terms of either the dinner or the show, and it is likely to be expensive. Popular clubs right now are the Blue Leopard at the Taprobane Hotel, the Little Hut at the Mount Lavinia Hotel and the Supper Club at the Hotel Lanka Oberoi. The usual nightclub performance consists of slightly plump girls doing a limbo dance and eating fire, and it is hard to say whether the girls or the patrons look more embarrassed.

Sports: Many clubs and associations provide facilities for golf, swimming, fishing, skin-diving, water-skiing, rowing, boating, yachting, tennis and yoga. Visitors may become temporary members. For golf, there's the Royal Colombo Golf Club and the Nuwara Eliya Golf Club in the heart of the tea country. Tennis and cricket enthusiasts can play at the Bloomfield Cricket and the Athletic Club. The Gymkhana Club, Nondescripts Cricket Club and the Women's International Club in Colombo.

Under-water Safaris in Colombo conducts under-water expeditions and supplies all types of diving equipment. It is based at Coral Gardens Hikkaduwa and at Alles Gardens, Sambative, six kilometers north of Trincomalee. The Poseidon Diving Station in Hikkaduwa hires all types of diving equipment while Beach Wadiya in Colombo provides facilities for skin-diving, spear fishing, rod and line and other water sports. Tourists wishing to sail should contact the Royal Colombo Yacht Club in advance as no taxi or tourist car may enter the harbor area without prior permission. Facilities for rowing, boating, fishing and yachting are provided by the Colombo Rowing Club and Ranmal Holiday Spot in Gorakana, Moratuwa. The Ceylon Angler's Club in Colombo specializes in inshore fishing. Two weeks' notice must be given for trout fishing. The Ceylon Sea Anglers Club in Trincomalee and the Sunstream Boat Services, National Holiday Resort in Bentota, both arrange excursions for deep sea fishing. The latter also arranges river cruises, trips in catamarans and sailing.

(above) A Colombo street scene.
(opposite page) Trained working elephants logging south of Ratnapura.

Regular bridge sessions are conducted by the Contract Bridge Association in Colombo. And for those interested in yoga, contact the Yoga Centre at Pettlai Road in Kalkudah.

Food and Drink in Sri Lanka

Sri Lankan cuisine always suffers somewhat in comparison with that of its nearest neighbor – India – which seems a little unfair. India, after all, is a mighty sub-continent with many regional varieties of food to offer, while its small cousin is just a modestly-sized island.

In fact Sri Lanka does have a pleasantly distinctive cooking style of its own, mainly built around the use of those spices which had Europe slavering at the door for so long. For those who like spicy food, there is plenty to enjoy in Sri Lanka once you know your way around the menu.

Unfortunately tourists can have quite a problem actually getting anyone to serve them real Sri Lankan food. It certainly is not offered in most hotels where tourists stay. Almost everyone in the tourist industry suffers from a reverse chauvinism which convinces them that no one from overseas wants their food. You can beg for good Sri Lankan food in most hotels and, even if they agree to bring it to you, it will arrive pale, uninteresting and almost without any spices in at all. The best solution is often to avoid hotel food and eat outside in a restaurant or rest house.

Pseudo-European food is offered to tourists throughout Sri Lanka and, sadly, it is often poorly cooked, poorly presented and totally unimaginative. Even breakfast is barely successful. All too often the only fruit offered – in this paradise of tropical fruits – is a banana or a slice of pineapple, followed by eggs, and more eggs. The idea that a tourist might conceivably not want an egg for breakfast has not yet occurred to most hoteliers.

The delights of real Sri Lankan food are:

Seafood – lots of it and fresh and cheap too. Avoid lobsters which tend to be expensive, but try trout, garoupa, fresh tuna, prawns, crabs, shellfish or seer (a fish rather like mackerel). Fish comes curried, fried, baked and dried. Tuna is prepared fresh, which is delicious. Dried tuna (called Maldive fish) is also used as a fragrant base to enrich a curry. Tuna is also the basis of a superb southern dish called *ambul thiyal*, which is originated in Galle and is fresh tuna baked with chilli and other spices into a rich hot dish. Definitely only for those who really like it hot!

Meat – tends to be buffalo (which is at best tender and tasty and very much like beef), beef, chicken, goat (also tasty, but has a slightly stronger flavor) and mutton. Probably the only pork will be found in Chinese and Christian households, if then. Meat dishes are usually curried, though steaks can be ordered in hotels.

String hoppers – of which the Sri Lankans are very proud, resemble noodles. They are made of rice flour, and generally eaten for breakfast. *Kiri hodi* is the name of the sauce poured over them.

Pan hoppers – these are flat little rice-flour pancakes cooked in a round pan, so they curve upwards. Most people tear them up and use them to scoop up curried dishes but as a tourist you can also get away with spreading butter and marmalade on them.they are often sold as street snacks and are cheap and delicious.

Egg hoppers – much the same as pan hoppers, but they have a fried egg tucked into the middle. They make a very tasty snack or a good breakfast dish.

Pittu – another common accompaniment to rice and curry. Pittu is rice flour and coconut cooked together in a bamboo tube. It is dry and crumbly after being steamed and is very easy on the stomach.

Short eats – consists of a plate of mixed snacks: spring rolls, pasties, samosas, sausage rolls and so on. It is found on most menus and is said to be a Western idea. You order what you want, paying only for what you eat.

Rice – nearly every tourist comments unfavorably on Sri Lankan rice. It is true that the rice, especially in the south, has an unpleasant, musty smell. Further north, however, you will find the problem disappears. One consolation: if you can bring yourself to ignore the smell, you will find the taste is fine. Also, most eating places – however high-class – do not seem to clean their rice very well and you would be wise to pick out anything that looks like a a stone before your teeth find it instead.

Lumprais (variously spelt). Now this is a happy marriage between Sri Lanka and colonialism. Said to have been started by the Dutch, this is a curry package steamed in a banana leaf. It contains steamed rice, vegetables, meat and egg all cooked together and makes a very tasty dish. Restaurants like the Green Cabin and Pagoda Tearoom in Colombo serve it and you can buy it in small eating shops in various towns along your route. It is not as hot as many other curries.

Rice and curry – these are the code words for lunch and dinner. Say them and you will be brought a whole selection of whatever is on the rice and curry menu that day. It will include rice, of course, probably a hopper or two, a meat, fish and several vegetable curries (unless you specify no meat, no fish), a dish of cooked lentils and some sambol. No one asks you which you want. It is assumed you want whatever they have and you can get more of any particular one for the same price. Do not be shocked by the size of the portions. You are not expected to eat it all. You could have rice and curry everyday for a month and it would never be the same.

Sri Lankans like their curries hot, so ask for medium or mild, if that is what you want. A good cook does not take out the tasty spices, he only modifies the chilli which is what makes the dish hot.

Sambol – this is very different from the South Indian sambal, so do not confuse the two. In Sri Lanka, sambol is fresh coconut grated up with chilli, with a little lemon juice added. Add it as you like to each mouthful of curry. Do not mix it in with the curry. This is the hot bit, so be careful. If you do take too much and your mouth is burning, do NOT drink water. Instead, eat a piece of sugar, take a soothing mouthful of curd and hold it in your mouth for a few seconds or chew a piece of fresh coconut.

Parippu – is a staple part of Sri Lankan diet. It is a dish of curried lentils which accompanies rice and curry and supplies good protein at low cost. It is also delicious.

Biriyani – a dish of Muslim origin, biriyani is rice cooked with stock and with vegetables added to the rice.

Sweets

The only real sweet to have with your rice and curry is curd and treacle (variously spelt tricul, treckle and so on). Curd is a yoghurt-like substance made from buffalo milk. It is deliciously cool and creamy. The so-called treacle is form the palm tree, and has pleasant taste, similar to maple syrup. The best comes from the kitul palm. It is thick and fudgy. This palm syrup is often called honey, but real bee's honey is rare and expensive.

Watalappam – an eggy pudding with raisins and fruits in it. Best made by Muslims, but probably introduced by the Portuguese.

(above) The back-breaking but picturesque labor of tending the rice paddies.
(opposite page) Ploughing the fields in the Kandy hills.

Jaggery – this is not exactly a sweet but it is incorporated into many sweet dishes. It is the dry, crumbly, and sugary lumps made from palm treacle. Used as sugar, it has a rich fudgy taste.

Kavun or kokis – a special New Year delicacy of rich oil cakes fried in coconut oil. Very tasty.

Fruit

Sri Lanka grows a great many tropical fruits but, due either to poor transportation or to bad organization, you hardly ever find each kind out of its own particular area. So, when you come upon a new kind of fruit, buy it because you probably will not see it elsewhere. Look out for roadside stalls as you drive along.

Banana – you may think a banana is merely a banana, but there are about 25 different kinds in this small island. They might be red-skinned; fat little yellow fingers sweet to eat; big fleshy plantains or green but ripe, so try them all. They are plentiful and cheap.

Coconut – the most prized coconut in Sri Lanka is the handsome king coconut, or *thambili*. It is golden-orange in color and Rugby ball-shaped. Its juice is sweeter than the green coconut, but it costs more and never has flesh inside. The ordinary green coconut is bigger, cheaper and may also have flesh to eat. These are for sale at roadside stalls and shops. After you have drunk the juice, get the green coconut split open by the vendor to see if there is flesh inside.

Mangosteen – this is a dark purple round fruit about the size of a fat plum, with sweet fleshy segments inside. It is grown and Kalutara on the southern road out of Colombo.

Rambutan – this is a hairy chestnut-colored small round fruit with the succulent flesh of the lychee inside.

Pineapple – found everywhere, and very cheap. You will be given it for breakfast until you hate it, then you will be given it for lunch and dinner.

Mango – there are 500 varieties of mango, but the best is said to be the Jaffna mango. Look for the big pink-cheeked one too.

Wood apple – this is a big, round apple-shaped fruit with an exterior as hard as wood. Sri Lankans love it and make it into drinks, jams and purees.

Jackfruit – think of a giant green hedgehog with no legs hanging from the trunk of a tree, and that is the jackfruit. Its spiky exterior protects a nest of seeds covered by yellow flesh which are sweet to eat and can be eaten raw as a fruit or cooked in a curry.

Durian – this less shapely cousin to the jackfruit – forbidden in hotels and on aeroplanes because of its curiously fetid smell – has a splendidly rich taste. It is said that if you eat too much ripe durian you will become drunk.

Papaya – also known as pawpaw, is a long marrowish looking fruit, green or orange on the outside with orange flesh within. It makes a good breakfast fruit and is said to be good for digestion and an uneasy stomach.

Guava – a tropical fruit more popular as a drink. It is hard and pear-shaped, with green skin tinged pink when ripe. It tastes distinctively sweet but is full of tooth-breaking seeds.

Drink

There is not a plethora of drinks to choose from in Sri Lanka, but with coconut like the thambili, this hardly matters.

Water – drink only water that you know has been boiled. If you are in any doubt about it, take no chances. Drink something else.

Tea – they may grow tea in Sri Lanka, but it is very questionable whether they actually know how to make it. Tea is almost always made very strong and you will probably need to order hot water with it. The exception to this is the roadside tea-stalls which make a pleasant glass of tea for a tiny charge.

Coffee – this is variable, but the best is a high-roast bean which makes a strong brew.

Soft drinks – it is hard to find cold drinks once you are out of the big towns, mainly because refrigerators are rare. The big towns boast a cold store or a cool house and these have soft drinks for sale straight out of the freezer in some cases. Coca-Cola is available, but the good local brand name is Elephant House. The lemonade is fair and the ginger ale and ginger beer are excellent and genuinely gingery.

Beer – local beer is a passable lager-style beverage, but it seems low in alcoholic content and is expensive. Good European lagers are available for just a little more.

Toddy – this is the real local brew and is a pleasantly winey alcohol collected daily from high up in the palm trees. If you look upwards along the southern coastal road early in the morning, you will see the toddy-tapper collecting the day's issue from the palm tree flower. It is slightly sweet, easy to drink and deceptively casual. A very big hangover could be possible from toddy.

Arrack – variously spelt, arrack is what happens to toddy when it grows up. It is distilled into this fiery brew of spirits. Some people make their own, which is illegal, but most buy it from the arrack store in the village. women, by the way, are not allowed to buy it. It can be very strong stuff indeed.

Colombo

"Colombo, as a town, presents little to attract a stranger. It possesses neither the romance of antiquity nor the interest of novelty," wrote sir James Tennent in 1864. Little has changed, as far as his comment goes, but there are places worth visiting.

Colombo has been a port from earliest times, but it did not become Sri Lanka's main port until the 1880s. The Moors used Colombo as a port of call from about the 8th century onwards. They came for cinnamon which they traded in Europe. They called the island Serendib, which successfully confused the Europeans for a long time.

The first written mention of Colombo came in 1330 from a Chinese traveler called Wang Ta-Yuan. This was not surprising as the Chinese had long established trade with Sri Lanka and some of the most numerous references to early Sri Lanka are to be found in Chinese. Wang called the city Kau-lan-pu, describing it as "a deep low-lying land, the soil poor, rice and corn very dear, and the climate hot."

There are numerous theories about the origin of the name Colombo. According to Tennent, the earliest form of the city's name was Kalan-totta, meaning the Kalany ferry which crosses the river Kalany-ganga. The Moors changed the name to Kalambu during their occupation of the beach and harbor in the 12th century. By the time the Portuguese arrived in the early 1500s, the name had become slightly altered to Kolamba or Columbu. The Portuguese, delighted that the name so closely resembled that of their star navigator Columbus, changed it to Colombo.

The city of Colombo was at first only a small local settlement tucked around the bay. The Portuguese built a little fort where the present landing jetty is located and they planned the layout of the streets. The

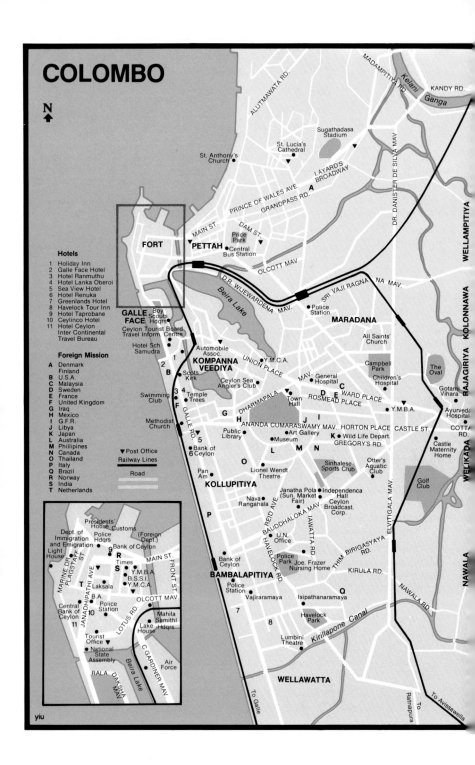

COLOMBO

N

Hotels

1 Holiday Inn
2 Galle Face Hotel
3 Hotel Ranmuthu
4 Hotel Lanka Oberoi
5 Sea View Hotel
6 Hotel Renuka
7 Greenlands Hotel
8 Havelock Tour Inn
9 Hotel Taprobane
10 Ceylinco Hotel
11 Hotel Ceylon
Inter Continental
Travel Bureau

Foreign Mission

A Denmark
Finland
B U.S.A.
C Malaysia
D Sweden
E France
F United Kingdom
G Iraq
H Mexico
I G.F.R.
J Libya
K Japan
L Australia
M Phillipines
N Canada
O Thailand
P Italy
Q Brazil
R Norway
S India
T Netherlands

▼ Post Office
Railway Lines

Road

yiu

city we see today was built by the Dutch and some of their best buildings still exist – Wolvendaal Hill Church, St Peter's Church in the Fort, the Pettah Post Office and the Dutch Museum.

Colombo became a commercial center when the British turned it into a big port in 1875, building a harbor wall to enclose it. Galle, shut out, ceased to be the main port of Sri Lanka and from then on all big business came to Colombo. The city has a population of nearly a million people distributed throughout the three main zones – Fort, the center of metropolitan activity, Pettah, the bustling bazaar area, and Cinnamon Gardens, now mainly known as Colombo 7, the fashionable residential area.

Sights of Colombo

Fort

Fort is no longer enclosed by fortified walls, as it was under the Portuguese, the Dutch and the British. It does have a couple of fat old cannons pointing out to sea, but that is about as martial as Fort gets these days. Banks, airlines and expensive shops are all to be found here.

The most important landmark in Fort is the Lighthouse Clock Tower, built in 1837. it was designed by Lady Ward, the wife of the then governor, and is probably the only lighthouse in the world in the middle of a city. The new (working) lighthouse is at Marine Drive (Chaitiya Road) overlooking the former Governor's Pool. A short distance from the old lighthouse is Janadhipathi Medura – the President's House, formerly the queen's House and home to the colonial governors of Ceylon. All of this area is spacious and rather grand, quite a contrast from the more active commercial streets of Colombo.

The statue beside the President's House is that of Governor Edward Barnes – known as the Great Roadmaker and responsible for the building of the Colombo-Kandy road. All mileage in Colombo is measured from this statue. Barnes was one of the adjutants of the Duke of Wellington at the Battle of Waterloo.

Overlooking the harbor in Fort is the Hotel Taprobane, which used to be known as the Grand Oriental. It still has the grand proportions and spaciousness of that bygone colonial era, but it no longer has the style.

At Gordon Gardens, next to the President's House, is a stately statue of Queen Victoria and a rock on which is carved the Portuguese coat-of-arms. Unfortunately the public is no longer allowed to enter Gordon Gardens as it is now enclosed in Republic Square where the President's and Cabinet offices are situated.

Just opposite the President's House is the General Post Office, a fine example of British colonial architecture. Look out for Cargills, the oldest department store in Fort. It opened in 1844 and stands at the junction of York Street and Sir Baron Jayatilake Mawatha. It has an old-fashioned air and seems to sell everything from hot water bottles to books. Nearby in the Australia Building is the government-run Laksala store, one of the most popular places to buy handicrafts and goods produced in Sri Lanka. The prices are fixed and reasonable and the range of goods is extensive.

The Central Y.M.C.A. can be found in Bristol Street, with the Moors Islamic Cultural Home as its next-door neighbor. One street away is the Young Men's Buddhist Association.

Worth a look, architecturally, are the two newspaper offices. The Times Building and Lake House. Lake House has a reasonably good bookshop offering a fairly wide range of books, as good as you are likely to get in Sri Lanka.

Pettah

Probably the most colorful area for tourists is Pettah. The word Pettah is Anglo-Indian, derived from the Tamil Pettai, and was a term used by the British to describe the part of town called by the Dutch Oude Stad, or Old Town. In Singhalese, this area is called Pita Kotuwa, meaning "outside the Fort". During Dutch times, this was a large bazaar where silks, materials and all kinds or foodstuff were sold. Some sections of Pettah were residential areas during the times of the Portuguese and the Dutch, and rich Burghers and Moors had their houses and warehouses here. Now the whole area is a giant bazaar, full of noise, shouting, ringing bicycle bells and all the tumult of a huge oriental market.

One striking feature is that shops selling the same type of merchandise tend to huddle together. This goes against most Western ideas of what makes good trade, but it happens throughout Asia and certainly does not seem to hinder trade. In Pettah there is an entire street – Sea Street – where gold is sold. In Gabo's Lane, a whole row of medicine shops sell traditional medicines derived from plants such as ginger to the more exotic medicines from animal by-products.

Give yourself plenty of time to wander around and don't be self-conscious. Many Sri Lankans are simply wandering around too, looking. Look at the trinket and jewelry shops where you'll probably find apprentices at work. Don't forget to look at the fruit and vegetable market at the end of Main Street.

While you are in Pettah, notice the different styles of architecture represented there – a legacy of the Moors, the British, the Dutch and the Portuguese. The belfry at Kayman's Gate once marked a section of Beira Lake. This end of the lake used to be inhabited by crocodiles (cayman in Dutch) and one legend says that the Portuguese used to feed their prisoners to the crocodiles. The old Pettah Post Office at First Cross Street was formerly a Dutch seminary, and in Keyzer Street you can still see headstones from the old Dutch cemetery. There are mosques and

Hindu temples (*kovils*) scattered throughout the bazaar area and down on the waterfront near Kochchikade is a Catholic Church dedicated to St Anthony the Miracle Worker.

Cinnamon Gardens

This is the smartest section of Colombo. It is everything Pettah is not – spacious, green and gracious. Known also as Colombo 7 (its postal district number), its name comes from the cinnamon plantation which once covered the entire area. This is a most attractive district, a small garden city where every large house stands in its own green surroundings, full of flowers, neat beds of plants and flowering shrubs.

There are several places of interest within Cinnamon Gardens if you are on a sight-seeing drive. The white-domed Town Hall, slightly reminiscent of St Peter's Basilica in Rome or perhaps even the White House in Washington D.C. is a grand and impressive building constructed in 1928.

Other places of interest are: the War Memorial commemorating the dead of two world wars; the Public Library; the Art Gallery, the Lionel Wendt Theatre and Art Centre; Colombo National Museum; Independence Commemoration Hall built in the style of ancient audience halls; the Bandaranaike Memorial International Conference Hall; and the Colombo Faculty of the University of Sri Lanka, which includes the Department of Aesthetic Studies. Next to the Bandaranaike Hall is an Anglican church which is an excellent example of modern ecclesiastical architecture.

For those who are interested in the arts, it is a good idea to check the daily newspapers t find out what performance or exhibition is being held at the Lionel Wendt Theatre and Art Centre. Much new young talent makes an early appearance there.

The Convention Complex which cost 30 million rupees to build features an octagonal style of architecture said to have been inspired by the architecture of the Kandyan period, but it looks more like one of the great mausoleum-like public buildings of Peking. The commemorative plaque relates that the Bandaranaike Memorial International Conference Hall was a gift to the people of Sri Lanka from the People's Republic of China. It stands in its own spacious grounds and is said to be one of the best convention centers in the South Asian region.

Open Spaces

Galle Face Green – Colombo's largest area of open space is Galle Face Green, which skirts the ocean for nearly a mile. It has a promenade built in 1859 by order of the then Governor Sir Henry Ward, in the "interests of the ladies and children of Colombo". The promenade still largely serves those same interests, attracting families to stroll in the cool of the day or on a sunny weekend.

Colombo, seen from Galle Face Green, looks like a slightly faded English seaside resort. Only the vigorous surf and the sentinel palms betray the fact that it is far from the English towns it imitates. One of the delights of the Green, which used to be known as the Hyde Park of Colombo, is to watch the kites flying there in the sunshine. The kites are made by Charlie Joseph, now nearing 70. He started making kites about 50 years ago, when they were all the fashion for those little colonial children being walked by their nurses. The children of those times have long gone but other children of many ages still queue up to buy Charlie's remarkable kites. The dancing birds and fish cost very little and are very popular but the most splendid of all is the 60-ft long dancing cobra.

Galle Face Green is the site of the **Galle Face Hotel**, one of Sri Lanka's oldest hotels (the oldest is the Queen's in Kandy) and certainly one of Asia's most stately hotels.

It was opened in 1864 when the Galle Face Green was at its most fashionable height. The hotel has a chequered career until quite recently, when it was acquired by the Regent international hotel group. They are gradually restoring the grand and imposing building to its former glory.

The hotel is directly in front of the rolling surf, and it also has its own swimming pool. It has a beautiful verandah and a first class seafood restaurant.

Vihara Park – The Vihara Maha Devi Park is in Cinnamon Gardens. It is a pleasantly landscaped collection of flowerbeds and lawns best visited from March to July, when most of the exotic shrubs are in flower.

At one end of the park, under the shelter of magnificent flowering trees, it an open-air theater.

The Royal Colombo Golf Club welcomes temporary members. It is situated on Model Farm Road, Colombo 8, but it only takes a few minutes to drive out to the 18-hole course.

Colombo Zoo is at Dehiwela, about 11 km from the Fort District. This is a spacious and well-landscaped zoo with an extensive collection of residents from tigers, bears, lions and elephants to different species of reptiles, birds, insects and fish.

For those who enjoy such spectacles, the elephants perform daily from 5 pm to 5.15 pm.

The zoo is open every day from 8 am until 6 pm. Admission fees are Rs.30 for adults and Rs.5 for children. Cars are charged Rs.5 and buses Rs.10.

Museums

The National Museum was set up in 1877 by the Governor, Sir William Gregory, whose statue now stands guard on the lawn. The museum has an impressive collection of antiques and *objets d'art,* and affords many insights into Sri Lanka's rich cultural heritage: sculpture from the ancient cities – including a very fine collection of Hindu and

A Buddhist ceremony in a Badulla temple.

Buddhist bronzes from Polonnaruwa; wood and ivory carvings; reproductions of temple frescoes; some fine china, especially of the Dutch trading days; and numerous other objects of interest, including coins and a good mask collection. Gifts received from visiting heads of state are also on display.

The museum also has a extensive library of half a million volumes, including 4,000 palm leaf manuscripts made from the ola (talipot palm) leaf.

The museum is at Sir Marcus Fernando Mawatha, Colombo 7, and is open from 9 am to 5 pm Sunday to Thursday. Adults pay Rs.20, children Rs.5.

The Dutch Period Museum is housed in a restored building in the bazaar area of Pettah. The restoration was paid for by a grant from the Netherlands. A special exhibition of life in Sri Lanka during Dutch colonial times is being held here, displaying objects from the Amsterdam Historical Museum, until the work on permanent displays is completed.

Temples

Colombo has a number of Hindu temples or kovils, even though the Hindu Tamils are somewhat in the minority in the south. Probably the best-known of all the Hindu temples are the old and the new Kathiresan, both of which are found in Sea Street in Pettah. It is from here that the Vel cart sets out on its journey during the festival of Vel, which takes place every July or August. The other kovils featured during this festival are two more Kathiresan temples situated along the Galle Road and another temple consecrated to Ganesh.

On Slave Island, in Kew Road, is a temple which used to be the favorite of the Indian Hindu soldiers brought into Sri Lanka by the British. It is the Sri Siva Subramania Swami Kovil.

In Kotahena Street is another kovil, the Sri Muthumariamman Kovil, dedicated to the Hindu goddess believed to be able to cure sufferers of diseases.

Three kilometers outside the Fort area is the Sri Ponnambala-vaneswarar Kovil, which is built entirely out of granite imported from Southern India. It is at Kortoboam Street, Kochchikade.

The most important of all Buddhist temples is the Kelaniyah Rajah Maja Vihara, an 11 km (6.8 miles) drive from the city. Local legend says that the Buddha himself visited this site and certainly its history has been recorded for the past 2,000 years.

Take a careful look at the paintings in this temple as they are among the finest of their kind that you are likely to see in Sri Lanka. They are comparatively new, it is true, but they have a splendid art nouveau style about them and the animals and birds are beautifully drawn and colored.

Attached to this temple is a small museum which has an odd collection of relics ranging from ancient parchments on religious matters to the Lord Buddha's bathing tub.

Kelaniya is an important center of Buddhist pilgrimage, and is the venue of the annual Duruthu Perahera held in January each year.

The Gotami Vihara, Borella, is notable for the contemporary paintings by George Keyt which adorn its walls. The paintings depict the life of the Buddha. The Isipathanaramaya, Havelock Town, and Asokaramaya. Thimbrigasyaya, also have paintings which illustrate the style of art during the Buddhist revival in the first quarter of this century. Gangaramaya, a training center for Bhikku and meditation, is located on a picturesque spot near Beira Lake. This center includes a museum of Buddhism. The Vajiramaya, Bambalapitiya, is one of the recognized seats of Buddhist learning and discipline. Buddhist sermons and discussions on Buddhist philosophy can be arranged here and at the Mettharamaya, also at Bambalapitiya. Just three kilometers out of the city at Kalapaluwawa is the Thapovanaya or "forest" hermitage, where Buddhist monks and laymen meditate in peaceful surroundings.

Mosques

As Colombo first became known as a trading place for the Arabs who were regularly visiting the small habor-side settlement as far back as the 13th century, it is not very surprising to find a thriving Muslim community even now. And where there are Muslims, there must be mosques.

The best-known of the mosques of Colombo are the Grand Mosque at New Moor Street; the Maradana Mosque at the Zahira College premises; the Devatagaha Mosque near the Town Hall at de Soysa Circus which is more than a hundred years old; and the very handsome Jami-Ul Alfar Jumma Mosque situated in the Pettah.

Churches

There are many churches in Colombo, all host to the dutiful, but some also of interest to those just passing through.

Probably the best known of these is the Wolvendaal Street, Colombo 13. It still holds services for members of the Dutch Reformed Church. This stolidly handsome church built by the Dutch dates back to 1749 and was consecrated in 1757. It is still in a very good state of repair and has a number of interesting gravestones inside and around the church itself. These were transferred to the church in 1813 and, for those who can decipher the Dutch inscriptions, they animate their own history.

Another particularly interesting relic of colonial times is St Peter's Church, near the Hotel Taprobane in Fort. This was originally part of the Dutch Governor's residence, and the present nave was a reception and banqueting hall. It was taken over by the British who first used it for Christian church services in 1804, and had it consecrated and dedicated to St Peter in 1812. Because of its historic interest, it is now preserved as an ancient monument.

There is also the Roman Catholic cathedral of St Lucia in Kotahena. Built on the highest point in the area it was completed in 1906, after 34 years of construction. The main nave of the cathedral can accommodate 6,000 people.

Eating in Colombo

You can of course stick to your hotel, but it would be a shame to miss some of what Colombo has to offer in the way of food. Try:

The Pagoda Tea Room, Chatham Street. A big, slightly shabby place popular with middle-class Sri Lankans. The food ranges from rice, curries, string hoppers, short eats and lumprais to various sweets and ice cream. Very modest prices, reasonably clean, and friendly service from the ancient waiters. Recommended.

The Green Cabin, Galle Road. This is a cousin to the Pagoda Tea Room. It is conveniently near the Tourist Board office too. Very good for lunch with good rice and curries, and a full range of Sri Lankan foods, plus excellent takeaway curries, samosas, curry puffs, buns and pastries. String hoppers available in the evening.

Palmyrah Restaurant, The Renuka Hotel, Galle Face Road. This, says the locals, is where you get the very best Sri Lankan food, but it is costly.

Seaspray, The Galle Face Hotel. Good seafood in the evening in an international standard hotel with a romantic setting – palm trees and surf. Service is excellent and the food costs much less than you might fear. Highly recommended.

The Tourist Board has approved these restaurants:

Western Food: Akasa Kade, Ceylinco House, Fort, tel: 20431-3. Green Cabin, Kollupitiya. Park View Lodge, Park Street, Colombo 2. Hotel Nippon Restaurant, 123 Kumaran Ratnam Road, Colombo 2. Pagoda Tea Room, 105 Chatham Street, Colombo 1. Ceyfish Restaurant, 1 Galle Face Centre Road, Colombo 3, tel: 26915. Sikoja, 25 B. De Saram Road, Mt Lavinia, tel: 071-5885. Le Cosmopolite, 20 Alfred Place, Colombo 3, tel: 26408.

North Indian Vegetarian Food: Saras Indian Vegetarian restaurant, near the junction of Duplication Road and Alfred Place, Colombo 3.

Sri Lankan and Oriental Food: Alhambra, Holiday Inn, Colombo 3. (Moghul food). Colombo North Restaurant, 140 Front Street, Colombo 11. The Taj, 11 Glen Aber Place, Colombo 3.

Light Refreshments: Gardenia Tea and Coffee Shop, Holiday Inn, Colombo 3. Pagoda Tea Rooms, Chatham Street, Fort. Perera & Sons, Colombo 3. The Rake, The Oasis Bar, Bamboo Bar, Green Cabin, Kollupitiya, Colombo 3.

Seafood: La Langousterie, Mt Lavinia. Seaspray, Galle Face Hotel, Colombo 3, tel: 28211/8. Sikoja, 25 B. De Saram Road, Mt Lavini, tel: 071-5885.

Chinese Food: Chopstick, 91/1 Havelock Road, Colombo 5. Hotel Nippon (also serving Japanese food), 123 Kumaran Ratnam Road, Colombo 2. Modern Chinese Cafe, 32 Havelock Road, Colombo 5. Nanking Hotel, Chatham Street, Fort, tel: 27888. Park View Lodge, 70 Park Street, Colombo 2. Chinese Lotus Hotel, Isabel Court, 265 Galle Road, Colombo 3. Colombo North Restaurant, 140 Front Street, Colombo 11.

Japanese Food: Kyoto Japanese Delicatessen, 19 De Vos Avenue, Colombo 4, tel: 83194.

Other Approved Restaurants: Blue Leopard, Fort. Palms, Inter-Continental, Fort. Flame Lanka Oberoi Supper Club, Colombo 3. The Emerald Tea and Coffee Shop, Fort. Coffee Shop, Colombo 3. Beach Wadiya, Colombo 4. Golden Topaz, Colombo 3. Chez Amano, Colombo 3. Eastern Palace, Colombo 3. Jade Gardens, Colombo 3. Flower Drum, Colombo 3.

Beach Resorts

Colombo has a sea-front extending 11 km (6.8 miles) south from Fort to Dehiwela, with many ideal places for sun and sea bathing, swimming and surfing. Just past Dehiwela is the beach resort of Mt Lavinia.

The Kandy Asala Perahera.

Mount Lavinia

Mount Lavinia, only 17 km (10.5 miles) from Colombo, serves as a holiday and weekend resort for those who live in the city. For tourists, its main attraction is certainly the Mount Lavinia Hotel, an old colonial-style residence converted into a stately hotel which commands the best view of the ocean.

There are many stories explaining the origin of this building, most of them entirely untrue. One says it was named after the wife of the Governor who had it built. In fact no British governor of Sri Lanka ever had a wife called Lavinia. It seems more likely that it is named after a certain local plant found in the vicinity, or "Lihiniyagala", meaning rock birds.

It would be a pity for visitors to miss the chance to visit a hotel which is both so beautifully designed and offers such good service. If there is not enough time to stay here, at least take afternoon tea.

There's more beach north of the city, at Hendala, which affords opportunities for boating along the old Dutch Canal which flows through miles of coconut groves.

Negombo

Negombo is a seaside resort 37 km (23 miles) north-west of Colombo. It is much vaunted as a holiday resort but it can't compare with the beaches of the south and east coasts. If you have only a day or so to see the sights out of Colombo, then Negombo will do, otherwise it may not be worth your while.

Nigumbo, as most Sri Lankans call it, became important under the Dutch. The Portuguese had done little with th place other than set up a cinnamon collection point there. The Dutch did little more for 150 years or so, but they appreciated it as the source of the best cinnamon in all the world. They fortified the town against the possible depredations of the Portuguese and they also built a canal which ran from Colombo to Negombo. Their fort still has its gateway, but little else, and you can see the date 1672 written above the entrance. The other thing Negombo is known for is its fish and the fishing folk go on unbothered by this modern age, just as they were unbothered by the coming of the Portuguese, the Dutch and the English. Many of them have been converted to Roman Catholicism and one offshore island, Duwa, puts on a Passion Play each Easter and the Pageant of the Three Kings (one of whom came from Jaffna, according to local tradition) at Christmas. There are so many Roman Catholics, in fact, that this area is called Little Rome.

If you like cricket, there is a match on the green by the Dutch fort every weekend in the season.

Going South

One of the most scenic routes in Sri Lanka is the coastal drive leading south from Colombo to Kalutara (known for its mangosteens and arrack); Beruwela and Bentota (tourist beach resorts); Ambalangoda (village of masks); Hikkaduwa (the cheap end of the tourist beach resorts, famed for its coral gardens and tropical fish); Galle (ancient port and superb fortified town with magnificent sea-facing ramparts); Weligama (home of the stilt fishermen); Matara (two smaller forts, one enclosing a village); Dondra Head (the Dondra lighthouse); Tangalla (fine beach and excellent accommodation); Hambantota (salt flats); Tissamaharama (excellent for bird-watching and wildlife); Kataragama (center for Hindu, Muslim and Buddhist pilgrims); and Yala (national park, with elephants, bears, leopards and other wildlife).

Once you leave the heavy traffic of Colombo behind, this road is an easy and pleasant drive past villages nestling in coconut groves. Here live the fishermen and the small farmers of the south. You see women making coir – the thick rope of coconut fiber – on what look like primitive spinning wheels. If you look skywards, especially early in the day, you will often see toddy-tappers strolling casually from palm to palm along overhead ropeways to collect the palm liquor without touching ground. Towards the end of the day, this is made into fiery arrack. Watch out for the toddy barrel carts, ox-drawn buggies with beautifully-made rattan arches shading the drivers.

There is plenty of accommodation along the way and at any price level you want; from big deluxe resort hotels to resthouses, small private inns and ordinary family homes. Often the best value is in the small private inns and homes. Sri Lankans are very hospitable and enjoy having paying guests. Their prices are usually very modest, their food beats any restaurant's and their houses are clean, comfortable and quite modern. Most have ordinary sit-down toilets.

It is not necessary to book ahead, except perhaps if you visit at the height of the tourist season; even then you can usually find somewhere to stay just by stopping in an area and asking around. If you want resort hotel accommodation, then you would probably be wiser to book in advance as hotels can be full from October to March.

Beruwela and Bentota

These have been included together since they are very close to each other. Beruwela is the first town and Bentota the next. Both are well-developed holiday resort with attractive surroundings and beaches catering for package tourists.

Beruwela was one of the towns where the Arabs used to call in their early trading days with Serendib. The name is a corruption of baeruala, a

Singhalese word meaning "the place where the sail was lowered". It is thought to have been the first Moorish settlement in Sri Lanka and still has a population of what are quaintly called Moors – people of Middle Eastern origin or, more recently, Indian Muslims who have emigrated to Sri Lanka. On the headland, there is a thousand-year-old tomb of a Muslim saint. A local legend says that a coffin made of rock floated to the headland and that it contained the body of the saint.

Bentota also boasts good beaches and reasonably, but not totally, safe bathing. In the 19th century, when most ships landed at Galle, it was the half-way stopping point between Colombo and Galle, and a coaching service ran between the two towns. Now it is known mainly for swimming and sunbathing, but the slightly adventurous can go upriver on a fishing boat – for a reasonably modest fee – and tease the crocodiles. There is also a 600-year-old Galapata Buddhist temple which has some good stonework.

Kalutara

Kalutara is proverbially the healthiest place in Sri Lanka, though its appearance – while pleasant enough – does not give open testimony to this. Some say it is the fresh air which blows there. This unassuming modern little town, divided by a smart bridge spanning the Kalu Ganga River, is known for its mangosteens, arrack and basket-work. The mangosteen is one of the most luscious of fruits, with a roundish appearance and a dark purply-black smooth outer skin which belies the sweetness of the flesh within. Numerous mangosteen stalls are found before and after Kalutara and the echoing cry of ". . . steeen" follows cars as they pass by. Don't pass them by. Stop and buy. Fruit is very regional, and only a few kilometers away there will be no more mangosteens to be had for love or money.

The basket-ware comes from the villages all around. Woven from the leaves of the wild date palm, the basic and ancient designs are mostly geometric patterns in red, black, orange and pink. If you are fond of baskets, buy here. The basket-ware you find in Colombo is not as good or as varied. This is also the place to buy a Panama hat.

All drivers – bus, car, lorry, or coach – stop at Kalutara to make a quick prayer call to the little Buddhist shrine beside the river. Meanwhile, you can look in at the Bodhi Trust Shrine across the road. This used to be the Government Agent's bungalow, but in 1960 it was endowed by philanthropist Sir Cyril de Zoysa and became a religious foundation. Upstairs you will find yourself inside a large sky-colored cupola, with a small white dagaba built within its center. The cupola is designed to produce echo and this has the interesting effect of turning every human murmur into a natural mantra. Round the inside of the cupola are consecutive illustrations of the Buddha's life. Some of the

Clothes being washed. They will be dried in the sunlight.

illustrations are bizarre, with an equally odd matching text. One of these says: "Queen elopes with legless person" and there portrayed is Her Majesty making off down the road with the legless person sitting on her shoulders, both of them looking remarkably cheerful.

From Kalutara it is possible to make some inland excursions to rubber plantations. All roads lead to one. Although little has endured to tell of it, Kalutara has had a colorful past. From very early days, Arabian traders used to take shelter there during the worst of the monsoons and later, during the times of the Dutch and the Portuguese, it changed hands so often that, according to Raven-Hart, "the inhabitants must have kept special notebooks to record whether they were then Dutch or Portuguese subjects". Kalutara was finally taken by the Dutch marching up from Galle in 1656. They besieged Kalutara fort for two weeks and after it surrendered through lack of food supplies, Colombo also fell and the Dutch were in command of Sri Lanka.

Looking out at the secure and prosperous-looking bazaar of Kalutara from the cupola of the Bodhi Trust Shrine, it is hard to realize how wild its past has been.

Ambalangoda

This sprawling village is the home of mask-making in Sri Lanka. Approaching its environs, the visitor sees masks everywhere – leering, threatening, grinning amiably from the verandah of practically every house and bungalow.

While many of these brightly colored masks are made strictly for the souvenir trade, there is more to mask-making than meets the eye. The masks are essential to the performance of complex dance rituals of unknown antiquity which play a vital role in village life, not just in Ambalangoda but in the rest of Sri Lanka.

There are two types of dances – the comic dance, called the *kolam*, and the devil dance.

The kolam is full of social satire and pointed political commentary and is usually performed once or twice a year for the general amusement of all. Kolam makes use of as many as 60 masks, but the expense involved in hiring the masks usually limits the number to around 21 per performance.

Devil dances are performed to drive out sickness, insanity, evil and supernatural presences. There are two kinds: *Raska* for exorcism and *Sanni* for sickness. In devil dances, the Eighteen Demons of Sickness form the basic cast. Again because of the expense, the entire cast is seldom seen. It is mainly the Demons of Death, Blindness, Deafness, Dumbness, Vomiting and Madness who contrive to appear most often.

Copies of the real masks used in the ritual dances are sold in Ambalangoda.

The master mask-maker is Ariyapala, an old man now in his eighties who can no longer see well enough to follow his craft. He is the fourth generation member of his family to make masks.

Ariyapala explained that a good mask-maker must also be a good dancer, since the virtues of each feed the other. He must also paint, carve, drum and sing.

Ambalangoda has a good beach and a small rocky island offshore worth inspecting. It also has a beautifully situated Rest House, commanding wide views of the beaches and with its own little rocky bathing pool. The Rest House started out as a storehouse during the times of the Dutch. *Areca nuts* (which people chew with green betel leaves, giving their mouths a startling red color) and cinnamon used to be stored here.

You can stay at the Rest House or at one of the many private houses which offer clean and inexpensive accommodation.

Hikkaduwa

After leaving Ambalangoda, the green land becomes arid. In certain seasons the tide sweeps inland and over the road itself, sometimes leaving a residue of red grit on the road surface.

A few kilometers before Hikkaduwa, there are some small villages where lime-making is the main cottage industry. The villagers collect limestone pebbles from the beach and pulverize them to sell to the flourishing local building industries. Although this produces extra income for the villagers, it tends to leave their villages looking grey and unattractive. The piles of limestone beside very house give them an oddly derelict look.

Hikkaduwa's shallow coral reefs just off the coast are much vaunted as a tourist attraction and they are beautiful and worth exploring. The flower-like corals and the iridescent technicolor fish which swim totally unafraid of the big clumsy humans invading their element are really splendid to behold. It is easy to swim out to the coral, but there is a treacherous undercurrent running off the shore. It is best to approach the main coral reef by swimming in a wide circular sweep from where most of the boats are moored, beyond the direct pull of the current. Any little boy will show you the easiest way to swim safely to the reef. There is a coral sanctuary near the shore fronting three "Coral" hotels, but there is more freedom to swim and explore further along near the Coral Gardens Hotel.

If you have never snorkeled before, this is your chance. It takes about three minutes to learn and straight away a startling submarine landscape is revealed.

Hunting and spear-fishing is prohibited so the fish are unafraid. Masks, flippers, and snorkel tubes can all be hired for a small fee from any hotel, whether you are staying there or not.

Glass-bottomed boats are also available for hire.

Weururakannale temple on the south coast.

Hikkaduwa has become the center for young travelers. It sports many small cheap hotels and restaurants, as well as shops which run up cheap cotton beach-wear in bright colors. It is the best place to shop for pants, tops, skirts, scarves and trinkets, but bikinis are rarer and disproportionately expensive.

If you have time, take a stroll through the village market. Piles of chillies, vegetables, fruit, dried fish and big fat tuna fish brought in from the sea twice a day all color the village scene.

Do not buy coral or even break it off yourself because a coral reef is a living thing and takes thousands of years to form. Coral once removed from the sea cannot be replaced. Marine experts say that the coral gardens of Hikkaduwa have been so badly plundered that it is perhaps already too late to save them.

Dodanduwa

The next small village along the coast is Dodanduwa, stretching out beside the sea and the palms. Unlike Hikkaduwa, it has escaped over-development and retains much of its natural beauty and peace.

As you drive along, watch for a sign on your left which reads *Sailabimbaramaha Viharayah, 1797*. If you are interested in seeing this old temple and the Island Hermitage where meditators seek a religious retreat, turn up the bumpy track. It stops at the foot of a Buddhist temple and Vihara. Up the steps – remember to remove your shoes first – you will find yourself in a typical country temple with a courtyard and small houses set into the wall under the green shelter of palm trees. The chanting of children from a nearby building indicates that this is a training school for young monks. The stately rise and fall of the ancient and sacred Pali tongue accords well with the atmosphere.

The temple's shrine room is painted from floor to ceiling with illustrations from the life of Buddha, probably dating from 1797 when the temple was built. Beside the large gilded Buddha is a smaller Buddha in white marble with a South Indian face. The Vihara is worth visiting. You might even get permission to go to the Island Hermitage, on the other side of the lake.

Koggalla

Koggalla is known for its fresh-water lake and the fact that it was an important naval airbase during World War II. Surrounded by sandy dunes and coconut palms, Koggalla boasts a fine hotel in the Koggalla Beach Hotel set by the edge of the sea. The bathing is safe and the beach is superb and well-guarded from hawkers and hustlers.

Weligama

Weligama (meaning "sandy village") is home fort to the stilt fishermen who sit on a single pole supported by a T-shaped spar, fishing with a line. For an hour or two, they perch on the shallow water just off the beach waiting for a yield from the sea. Why they should fish in this picturesque and peculiar way nobody seems to know. One suggestion is that shoals do not gather like those in Hikkaduwa, another that the shallow water precludes more conventional methods.

Weligama, like the rest of the coastal towns stretching down to Hambantota, was an important part of the ancient kingdom of Ruhuna. The language, customs, history and ethnic background of the people were entirely different from those who lived in the North. They are said to be the most purely Singhalese. It was in the temples and viharas of the south that scholarship was preserved, and even today some claim that the most learned of the monk scholars are to be found in this area.

It is also one of the most attractive stretches of coastline, edged with coconut palms and deckled with hundreds of little bays and inlets cut by the wash of the sea.

At the outskirts of Weligama are pottery stalls offering a collection of red clay pottery and Hindu deities. These stalls are very popular among Indian tourists. There are some red clay oil-lamps which would make handsome plant- or candle-holders, but they are over-priced, so bargain hard.

There is a fork in the road leading to Weligama. The main road goes inland and the coastal road leads to a picturesque little island on which stands a villa, just off the coast near the Rest House. The octagonal villa is owned by writer Paul Bowles. In an excerpt from Bowles' article "How to Live on a Part-Time Island", he writes; "According to the deed the original name of the little hump rising out of the sea was Galduwa, a Sinhalese word meaning 'rock island'.

On the island road the only real point of interest is the Kustarajah Statue standing at the corner of the junction. It is a Buddha-style statue lent a slightly sneering look by a broken nose and damaged mouth for which the Portuguese soldiers were responsible some four hundred years ago.

Much myth surrounds the origins of the statue but experts say that the statue is that of the Bodhhisatva Avalokiteshwara, "the Compassionate One", one of the incarnations in the Mahayana Buddhist sect, and dates from the 9th or 10th century.

Across a field on the opposite side of the road from the Kustarajah Statue is the Agrabodhi Temple. Within is a 400-year-old Buddha statue which was gilded until the Portuguese stole the gilding from it. There are ceiling paintings portraying heaven, three-dimensional statues, and a great *trompe d'oeil* painted balcony with stage curtains around a hundred-year-old painting of scenes from the Buddha's life.

There is also a Lord Vishnu statue in the Buddhist temple. To the purely Buddhist, this may seem like a form of religious decadence. The Singhalese, however, explain that since the early kings of Lanka married Hindu princesses, they allowed Hindu statues in their temples as a courtesy. This is common all over the south.

Weligama also produces some excellent lace-making and some pottery which is more desirable than the crude red clay variety. Dutch-style architecture is very much a feature of this area.

Galle

Galle is a strikingly attractive place, with a number of unusual features. The most outstanding of these are the great walled ramparts now lined with grass which enclose the ancient city of Galle, leaving the featureless new suburbs outside.

From earliest history, Galle was famous as a trading center. It served as an entrepôt where the Moorish traders of Malabar met up with the Chinese junks and bought from them their cargoes of silk, gems and spices. Historians say that all the ancient sailors – the Persians, the Egyptians, the Greeks and the Romans – came to Galle long before the arrival of the Moors. It is even suggested that Galle is the Tarshish of the Bible, to which Solomon sent for the jewels which helped him to win the heart of Sheba.

Up to 120 years ago, it was still possible to see a fleet of different vessels from various parts of the world – Arab dhows, ships from Malabar, dhoneys of Coromandel and, of course, the outrigger canoes of the Sri Lankan fishermen. Only the outrigger canoes remain.

The name Galle is probably a corruption of the Singhalese *gala* meaning a resting place for bullocks. Some experts claim that it is derived from another Singhalese word with the same spelling but a different pronunciation, which means a rock. There are rocks in the harbor which often proved hazardous and even fatal to the ships that used the harbor for shelter. The coat-of-arms of Galle bears a heraldic pun, a crowing cock – cock being *gallus* in Latin.

Despite the numerous modernizations and changes which have been made to the old buildings inside the fort. Galle still retains an atmosphere very much its own. The narrow streets still bear Dutch names. The thick strong walls surround and protect spacious and lofty houses in the Dutch style, with cool verandahs and shady courtyards, many of them quite well preserved.

Likewise many of the current administrative buildings date from the Dutch era, as does a sophisticated sewage system with huge, brick-lined underground sewers which were automatically flushed out by the tide twice a day. The Burghers even put to profitable use the little musk shrews which bred in the sewers by exporting them to Europe for use in the perfume trade.

The buildings on Hospital Street now used by the government were once the Dutch hospital and factory. Another notable structure is the Walker's Office, which many think is the finest old building in Galle. It was originally the Commander's Office and later, under British occupation, it became known as the Queen's House. One British administrator, Campbell, said it was haunted by the Von Hegel whose spurs now hang in the new church . Campbell was responsible for planting many of the trees and shrubs which make Galle so attractive now.

There are a couple of unimposing English churches, which are interesting relics of their time. It is also well worth taking a good look at the old gateway to the fort. Dated 1669, it is a sturdy structure, well able to withstand a battering ram or two. On the monogrammed shield are the letters V.O.C., which stand for *Vereenigde Oost Indische Campagnie*, or United East India Company. There are also Dutch trading tokens with the same initials to be found all over Sri Lanka and which can be bought for a modest sum.

Most of the British contributions to this bustling Burgher town were more peaceable. Until Colombo's artificial harbor was built in the 1870s, Galle was the main port of Sri Lanka. Even as late as 1893, a new passenger jetty was built. Because of this, it was home for a number of foreign merchants who built magnificent mansions there, houses like Closenberg, Eddystone, Mt Aerie, Mt Pleasant, and Armitage Hill. Closenberg has been made into a hotel, and it is highly recommended by those who have stayed there for its antique furniture and fittings, its period atmosphere and its hospitality.

Images of Buddha in the Matara saves.

There are numerous private houses in Galle offering accommodation for reasonable prices. The Closenberg is at the other end of the scale but, if you can afford it, it is worth it.

Things to buy in Galle include hand-made lace, a craft handed down by the Portuguese. There are no lace factories; instead you see old and young women sitting in their doorways painstakingly doing the fine, web-like work. There are also tortoise-shell wares and carved ivory, but these products come from protected species and therefor it is technically an offence to buy them. You won't be able to export them either.

Matara

The main town of modern Matara, the terminus of the southern railway, is big, bustling and sprawling. It is also the point at which the river Nilawala Ganga joins the sea. The real point of interest is in the old part of town where there are two ancient Dutch forts.

It was the Portuguese who originally fortified the town in 1550 when they helped King Dharmapala build a fort. However, the buildings which you see today date from 1645 and were erected by the Dutch when they took the town from the Portuguese.

Although Galle is probably the most famous of the fortified towns, Matara has much character and charm. The fort houses a whole village as well as a Rest House. Within the broken-down ramparts are a clock-tower and two courts – a High Court and a Magistrates' Court,

Outskirts of the old town in Matara.

which probably accounts for the number of attorneys' offices on the streets. The lanes are tree-lined, and grassy walks lead right to the sea. On one side of the fort is a lagoon. For a small fee, the boatmen can be persuaded to take you around the lagoon which teems with marine life – huge water monitor lizards and numerous water birds.

The Star Fort, once handsome, is now in a state of decay. It is made of coral, and is very small. There is a notable archway entrance above which is a coat-of-arms and the name Redoute Van Eck, 1765. Van Eck was the Dutch governor at that time. Inside the thick walls is a wooden building which was once used as a public library. In a room entitled Reference there are some hideous wall paintings of animals and birds. Walking around the walls, the course of a small moat, now dried out, is still visible.

Outside the fort are the curd-and-treacle stalls. Matara is famous for its curd, a yoghurt-like dish which is eaten with a topping of palm syrup similar in taste to maple syrup.

Matara used to be the hub of the spice trade. It was also used as a health center for soldiers of the Galle Fort.

The best place to stay is the historic Rest House, a pleasant bungalow overlooking the sea, said to be sited on an old elephant corral where elephants were kept before they were exported.

Matara is also the source of the so-called "Matara diamonds" which are actually semiprecious zircons. You would do well to avoid buying gemstones from street hawkers unless you are prepared to over-pay.

From Matara it is an easy inland journey to two monuments of particular note: Weherehena and Udagama. Reaching Weherehena entails a drive past lagoons and across red earth that contrasts with the enveloping green of the jungle.

The Weherehena Vihara features a 39-m (128 ft) high Buddha painted in bright red and yellow. As an example of the modern style of statuary it differs greatly with the fine early Buddhist statuary. The monument is a haunt for tourist and intensely commercialized – even the monks come out and ask for pens! Visitors are taken to an underground building, through a series of corridors painted from floor to ceiling with dark pictures, and down to a special shrine room said to contain relics of the Buddha. The relics are viewed from reflections in a mirror as it is considered a sacrilege to display them directly. Visitors are asked to give a donation.

Udagama has a vihara set amid a plantation of cinnamon trees, with the white dagaba and a serene tree-edged courtyard. It is located on the road going back towards the coast.

Living in the vihara is the Reverend Buddarakkita, famous in Sri Lanka for his healing prowess. Villagers from far and wide who would rather seek traditional herbal treatment than go to a modern hospital travel to Udagama to get medical attention from the monk. Bone-setting is his specialty. With the use of massage, special oils and herbal medicine; he is able to set broken bones so that they heal without leaving any permanent damage, stiffness or shortening of the affected limb. He is very famous, and several foreigners have gone to him for treatment.

Like most doctor-monks he learned his craft from the ancient Pali texts which detail the traditional methods. He grows herbs, trees, spices and shrubs for his medicines, including cinnamon, and he makes special oils which he uses as a base for his various balms.

At the Udagama Vihara there is a strong sense of the seeming innocence which leads people mistakenly to see the life as a retreat from the world. If you want to wash off the taint of commercialism from shrines like Weherehena and would appreciate peace and dignity, visit Udagama.

Dondra Head

The coastal road to Dondra Head, southernmost part of Sri Lanka, opens right out to sea.

The little town with the lighthouse has few attractions, apart from a Victorian-style Devinuvara Vishnu Temple, and it is to the lighthouse itself that you should go. Built in 1889, the 52-m (170 ft) high lighthouse looks out over the sea and is a good place to sit and meditate.

Today there is just the sea, the lighthouse, and the leafy green lanes leading to the lighthouse, full of children who ask for money or pens or sweets. Each year, pilgrims visit Dondra Head for a big perahera and fair.

On the road south from Dondra, cashew-nut sellers roast cashews beside the road. When you see the cashew nut in its natural form, you will understand why they are so expensive. The cashew is a kernel in the center of a large pear-shaped fruit which is used mainly in medicines. fumes from the burning on its skin act as a mosquito repellent.

If you want to visit the other giant Buddha from Dikwella on the coastal road, it is necessary to cut inland to Beliatta. On the Beliatta road and a short distance further along, you will see the Werukannala Vihara. If you have a sense of deja vu, it is because it bears a remarkable similarity to the vihara at Weherehena.

The 40-m (131 ft) tall Buddha – the height of a 10-story building – is claimed to be the biggest Buddha in Sri Lanka. To prove it, there is an actual 10-story building behind it. You can climb up to the Buddha's head and see all the Buddhist scriptures on a little brass plate inside the head.

Tangalla

Back through the largely Muslim town of Dikwella and on the coastal road again, the next major town is Tangalla. Tangalla is known for its beautiful beaches and hinterland of shady green lanes and houses with gardens leading to the sea. There are some Dutch buildings in the town and the Rest House used to be the Dutch Administrator's house.

The necklace of little bays around Tangalla make it an excellent stop for lazing in the sun. Some of the bays are subject to treacherous currents and can be risky for swimming, but the bay on the town side of the Tangalla Bay Hotel is generally safe. Beside the Rest House is another bay, safe but rather shallow.

If you want to spend more time in Tangalla, take a lagoon tour in an outrigger canoe or catamaran. This kind of trip is easy to arrange and costs very little. The water of the lagoon is dark green, overhung in many places by drooping trees, trailing twiggy branches in the water. Kingfishers can be seen in profusion, and scaly water monitors with tongues flicking in and out like snakes swim across the water. These ungainly dragon-like lizards thrive on all that decays. *Kirala Mal*, the bottle-top tree, grows in the lagoon. It is so called because its roots stick up through the water and can be cut and used as bottle stoppers once they have dried out. Fresh water prawns live in the lagoon too and fishermen use small catamarans to track them down.

If you want a side trip before Tangalla, Hulugalle's guide recommends following the minor track back to Nakulugamuwa. This is a small village with sheltered bay dominated by cliffs. Nearby is an underground cave which connects with a vertical tunnel through which the water roars up to the cliff to a height of 18 m (59 ft).

Hambantota

After leaving Tangalla, the countryside changes dramatically. It loses the soft green look of the southern coastal road, quickly becoming drier and more fierce. Scrubby bushes replace the flowering shrubs. Fields are wider and get rougher until you reach the scrubby sparse countryside of the Yala Park area.

Hambantota is the end of the trail for the southern coastal road. From here, you can go inland and north to the hills, east to the game parks or the east coast. But it is th end of the southern trail.

Off the town are some superb beaches, long and smooth. For the greater part of the year it is the gathering place of the outrigger fishing boats. Many of these boats head for the east coast in August, following the schools of fish. Otherwise Hambantota is of interest for its salt pans. Sea water is allowed to dry out in shallow lagoons until the salt crusts along the edges of the water. This time-honored method of making salt gives a bleached-out look to the land.

Apart from salt-making, the main local occupation is fishing for crabs, lobsters and crayfish.

A large part of the population is made up of Malay Sri Lankans. They are the Muslim descendants of Malay soldiers once employed by the Dutch and British governments.

Kataragama

The road eastwards leads to Kataragama, going first through Tissamaharama, "Tissa's Great Temple". On one side of the road is a tank, on the other some superb dagabas. This is an area of many delights for bird-watchers and, fortunately for them, there is also an excellent Rest House just near the tank. The quiet rural peace of the area is enhanced by the luxuriant paddies all around.

Kataragama is one of the holiest places in Sri Lanka for Hindus, who travel there to worship the Hindu god of war. Kataragama (also known as Skanda or Kartik). There are also important Buddhist and Muslim shrines and the whole area is sacred. A new temple complex now exists there, with special compounds for the Buddhist and Muslim shrines. Large sums of money have been invested for its development as a religious zone of ecumenicalism (excluding only the Christians and Jews who are not represented by a shrine), but it has a somewhat grubby appearance which is unlikely to make it attractive to ordinary tourists. For religious pilgrims, however, it is the center of constant attention, culminating in a *perahera* or religious procession in June during which all kinds of ceremonies and rituals can be seen, including fire-walking.

In the evening there is an interesting little fair of numerous stalls, selling beads, pictures and incense, as well as tasty snacks. There are pilgrim rest houses at which tourists are allowed to stay. They are clean and cheap and offer good vegetarian food. No alcohol is allowed on the premises.

The Ancient Cities and the Cultural Triangle

The term Cultural Triangle is much bandied about in Sri Lanka now and it refers to conservation projects in Anuradhapura, Polonnaruwa and Kandy, the three cities of the Triangle. These particular cities have been chosen because of their significance in the history of Sri Lanka.

Anuradhapura, with its artificial lakes, monasteries, imposing stupas and pleasure gardens, was the first capital of Singhalese Buddhism. The next capital was Polonnaruwa, with its fortified walls surrounding sanctuaries dominated by the carvings of Gal Vihara – a huge reclining Buddha – set amid parks watered by the reservoirs built by the great King Parakrama Bahu. Kandy (see HILL COUNTRY), the last capital, is now the center of Buddhism, with its Temple of the Tooth. This is the triangle of Sri Lanka's twin achievements – Buddhism and building.

Many of the ancient monuments are still to be seen and are still impressive. However, the ravages of time and climate have left most of them in need of care and restoration. Preservation work, which is time-consuming, is still going on at the sites.

Anuradhapura

Many visitors find their first visit to Anuradhapura, the mightiest of the ancient cities, disappointing. This is largely because the constant use of the term "city" leads people to expect a thriving metropolis. Instead

Ratnaprasada temple in Anuradhapura.

they find ruins, fallen temples and unidentifiable mounds scattered over a radius of 80 km (50 miles). Anuradhapura, however, is still considered a sacred city.

It was founded as a capital in 380 BC and in its heyday was visited by pilgrims and merchants who came from all over Asia to see its marvels. Its decline came before the 10th century when the jungle first encroached upon the city and slowly devoured it, though it did continue to attract some pilgrims. Much of it remained buried until the British became interested in it archaeologically and started excavating and restoring the buildings.

Life in Anuradhapura intensified with the invasion of Sri Lanka in the 6th century BC by a band of Aryans from North India, led by Prince Vijaya who became the first king of Lanka. They landed on the west coast and made their way inland where they settled through conquest, marriage and local alliances.

The city was a splendid piece of planning. According to the Great Chronicle, the king laid out precincts for huntsmen, used 500 cleaners to clean up the city, 200 to clean the sewers, and 150 to carry away the dead. He built a monastery for wandering medicant monks, a hermitage for ascetics, a house for pregnant women, and a hall for those recovering from sickness. He ensured a water supply by having tanks built and he made sure there were dwellings for untouchables, heretics and foreigners.

The king's grandson, King Devanampiyatissa, was to witness an event which profoundly changed the nature of Sri Lanka. This was the advent of Buddhism. According to the Great Chronicle, great wonders occurred at the king's consecration. "In the whole isle of Lanka, treasures and jewels that had been buried deep rose up to the surface of the earth."

Then in the year 307 BC the great monk Mahinda arrived in Sri Lanka, charged with the sacred duty of converting Lanka to Buddhism. Mahinda was the son of the great Buddhist Emperor, Ashoka.

After they met Mahinda decided that King Devanampiyatissa would be a suitable candidate for conversion. This much-quoted and obviously subtle conversation followed:

"What name does this tree bear, O king?"

"This tree is called a mango."

"Is there yet another mango besides this?"

"There are many mango trees."

"And are there yet other trees besides this mango and the other mangoes?"

"There are many trees, sir: but those are trees that are not mangoes."

"And are there, besides the other mangoes and those trees which are not mangoes, yet other trees?"

"There is this mango tree, sir."

This convinced Mahinda of the king's intellectual worth and he converted the king and his court, after which the rest of the people soon followed. This started a period of construction. Temples, dagabas, monasteries and other shrines were built, laying the foundations for Anuradhapura.

The king sent for a branch of the Bo Tree under which the Buddha himself attained enlightenment. According to the Great Chronicle, the branch severed itself and was brought on a great gold chariot into Anuradhapura. Within a few days it had rooted and sprouted new shoots. That tree can still be seen today, 2,200 years later. It is the oldest known tree in the world, since the original Bo Tree was cut down many centuries ago. Even during the years of the city's obscurity, the Bo Tree was always the object of pilgrimage as it is now.

For the next few centuries, visitors continued to visit the great city from the farthest corners of Asia. Many of them, fortunately, recorded their experiences and it is through their eyes that we can still see something of what the sacred city was like at the height of its prosperity.

One of these travelers, the Chinese pilgrim Fa Xian, has left us a particularly vivid account. Fa Xian was a devout Buddhist and he came to Sri Lanka in search of religious texts which were not available in newly-converted China. He took the long overland route, making his way through the Gobi Desert, across the Himalayas, to India and then by boat to Sri Lanka. He arrived in Anuradhapura in 414 and lived there for two years.

"The dwellings of the merchants are very grand," he wrote. "And the side streets and main thoroughfares are level and well-kept. At all points where four roads meet, there are chapels for preaching the faith."

He refers to the Tooth Relic, which is now in Kandy, but which originally rested at Anuradhapura, and described the riches of the Abhayagiri Dagaba and Monastery – the institute endowed by the heretic King Dhutta Gamani.

"There are five thousand monks. There is in it a hall of Buddha, adorned with carved and inlaid work of gold and silver, and rich in the seven precious substances, in which there is an image (of the Buddha) in green jade more than twenty cubits high."

Anuradhapura continued to be the capital until 992 AD, when King Mahinda V abandoned the city under duress from the constant invasions and attacks of Tamils from South India. The new capital became Polonnaruwa, which was better protected from invaders by the surrounding mountains.

Seeing Anuradhapura

There is not much to see in the sacred city. Many people relegate this city to a drop-in trip but the experience is meaningless. Far better to spend two or three days here. There are two excellent guest houses, the **Nuwarawewa** in the new city and the **Tissawewa** in the ancient city.

These are privately run, reasonably priced, and present good food and service. The advantage of the Tissawewa is that it lies within the ancient city and has a beautiful garden surrounding it. It is a cleverly converted old Dutch house which retains the style of times past: a superb verandah, a stately dining room, waiters in white gloves and antiques throughout.

If you are not too unathletic, you can hire a bicycle for a very modest fee and ride around the ruins at your own pace. Be wary of hiring local guides. Many of them talk rubbish and you will be paying merely for a story-telling session. They know nothing about the city and bank on the fact that you don't either. Another warning: do not be deceived by the wandering antique hawkers. On the whole they do not have a real antique within a hundred years of their stock and their prices are grossly inflated.

What to See

The Sri Mahabodhi Tree: (See p.18 for the historical context in which the tree is planted.) The sacred tree is in its own compound, surrounded by golden railings and propped up by supporting poles. It has become so frail that there are notices requesting people not to burn camphor and incense as offerings, as the fumes may harm the tree. Flags denoting vows and promises made, prayers and requests granted, bedeck the tree.

The Bo Tree as a species propagates with underground roots that develop as apparently new saplings, but which feed off the same trailing roots. An ancient tree such as this would have roots that are likely to extend for at least a mile all round, and therefore every bo tree within a mile of the sacred Bo Tree is actually part of it. Some Buddhists find this hard to accept.

If you can, time your visit so that you are in Anuradhapura during the full moon, or Poya. There are three nights of full moon and on each night there are special ceremonies at the Bo Tree. People coming from many miles around with their offerings and evening food camp out on the hard ground of the courtyard. The whole night is spend in prayer, meditation, listening to the reading of the Buddhist Sutras by the monks and perhaps just sleeping in the shadow of all this holiness. It is a moving sight. Old ladies curl up quite happily on the ground, whole villages may make a pilgrimage together and offer a thousand butter lamps in the shape of a yantra. If you wear all white clothing, you may even go up into the shrine of the Bo Tree. A visit at this time will do more to convey the power and peace of Buddhism than a hundred books or a score of visits to old ruins.

The Brazen Palace: This was built by King Dhutta Gamani as an offering to the monks. Obviously a magnificent structure, the Great Chronicle describes it as such:

"It was four-sided, [measuring] on each side a hundred cubits and even so much in height. In this most beautiful of palaces there were nine

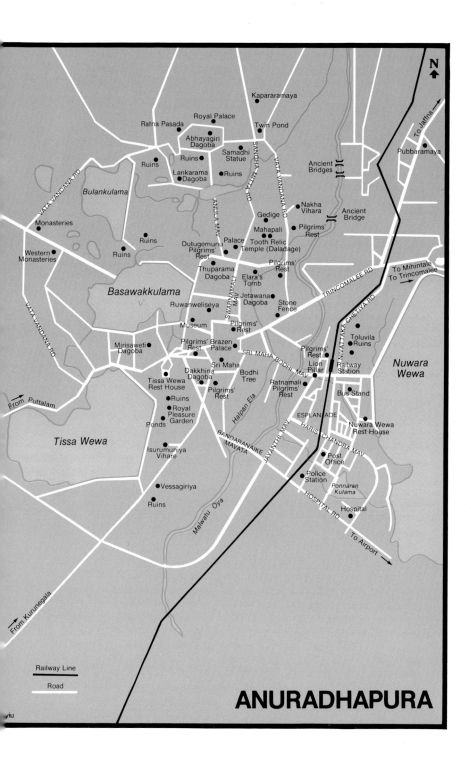

ANURADHAPURA

storys, and in each story a hundred window chambers. All the chambers were overlaid with silver and their coral balustrades were adorned with manifold precious stones, gay with various gems were the lotus flowers on the balustrades and they were surrounded with little silver bells".

However, all this came to nothing about 15 years later when the whole palace burned down, leading to the assumption that its main structure was wooden. The 1,600 pillars of stone which now mark the site were no part of the original building. They were added much later, during the reign of King Parakrama Bahy I (1153-1186).

The Thuparama Dagaba: This is the oldest Buddhist edifice to be found in Sri Lanka and it is known as a stupa (in Pali, it is *thupa*; in Singhalese *dagaba*). *Dagaba*, also anglicized as *dagoba*, literally means a relic chamber, but it has come to mean the edifice which encloses a relic chamber. The Thuparama Dagaba was built by King Devanampiyatissa (250-210 BC) to house certain relics of the Buddha. These were the collar bone of the Buddha and the tooth relic.

The present bell shape of the Thuparama dates back only to its restoration in the 1840s. It has long been the habit of pious and wealthy Buddhists to undertake restoration of religious monuments, but unfortunately the restoration was usually in the form of the latest religious fashions and not done with any regard for the actual archaeological details of the building. Their piousness often causes grief to the more purist archaeologists.

Originally, the stupa was of the so-called paddy heap shape and the pillars which surround it once upheld a circular room. This circular relic house, or *vata dage*, is a typically Sri Lankan architectural feature.

The Abhayagiri Dagaba and Monastery: Giri, a hermit, made a bad move the day he saw the defeated King Vattagamani Abhaya and called after him scornfully: "The great black lion is fleeing!" Unfortunately for Giri, the king's fortunes recovered, his troops overcame the Tamil invaders who had chased him off his throne 14 years earlier and one of the first to know it was Giri. King Vattagamani Abhaya was not one to forgive easily. He destroyed Giri's hermitage and raised up the Abhayagiri Dagaba and Vihara on the same spot. The name is a marriage of the king's name and the hermit's. It also contains an assertion of non-cowardice – Abhayagiri means Mountain of Fearlessness.

The building is the second largest stupa in the world. It is 114 m (374 ft) high and remarkable in terms of engineering skill and architectural achievement.

The stupa forms part of the UNESCO Cultural Triangle project in Sri Lanka which is to restore certain major architectural and religious sites of prominence. The greater part of the stupa is still buried and it is planned to excavate it. The project started in 1981 and already visitors can see some beautiful examples of early statuary being unearthed. Restoration work is still going on and will take several more years to complete.

The Samahdi Buddha: This 4th-century carving is considered to be one of the masterpieces of Buddhism and shows the Buddha in meditative pose. You will notice that the Bo Tree behind this statue is dying.

The Ruvanvali Dagaba: The superb, white-domed Ruvanvali Dagaba, with its golden pinnacle catching and reflecting the rays of the sun, dominates the countryside around Anuradhapura. When King Dhutta Gamani decided to build this great stupa (c. early 1st century, BC), he summoned the master builders and asked them in what form they would like to build it.

He build a 90-m (295-ft) high dagaba with a superb white dome protected by a wall of 336 elephants, each unique and individually carved. Unfortunately the building we see today is not the perfect half-globe of crystal. Modern engineers, doing restoration work at the behest of the Buddhist Union, had to flatten the shoulders of the dome, so it lost its rounded shape. Soon after the restoration, the crystal jewel which was donated by the Burmese to crown the pinnacle was struck by lightning and shattered.

It is said that when King Dhutta Gamani was dying, with the Ruvanvali still incomplete, he instructed his brother to finish the work. His brother, understanding that the king was saddened by having failed to finish the great stupa, had a model cunningly constructed and painted which fooled his brother into thinking that his life work was actually finished.

The Jetavanaramaya: This 120-m (394-ft) high stupa built in the 4th century AD was at the time the largest stupa in the world, surpassed in size only by two of the pyramids of Giza. It is still the largest stupa in Sri Lanka, built by King Mahasena the heretic for the sect of monks he favored.

The rough brick surface is more faithful to the original appearance of the stupa. There is very little description of the building in the Great Chronicle, as King Mahasena had bitterly alienated the writers who were themselves orthodox Buddhist monks.

The total restoration of the Jetavanaramaya being undertaken as part of the UNESCO Cultural Triangle project is estimated to take several years to complete.

Kuttam Pokuna: These recently restored twin bathing ponds are considered to be among the best works of this kind in the sacred city. They belong to the Abhayagiri Monastery.

Other sights: The road which goes north runs through the site of the royal palace, the **Sangamitta Mawatha**. This was built in the 11th century AD by King Vijaya Bahu in the royal capital of Anuradhapura after the city had fallen, perhaps to try to keep the city for his own. Near this site is an old well and the **Mahapali**, the Monks' Refectory. You will see a huge trough, like a giant horse-trough. This used to be filled with boiled rice which was dished out to the monks.

Mahasena's Palace can be found beyond the Abhayagiri Monastery. It is largely in ruins, but is notable for having the finest moonstone to be found in Anuradhapura. To the permanent frustration of photographers, the railings which surround this moonstone make it impossible to take a picture without that shadow falling on it somewhere. The moonstone – nothing to do with the gem – is a half-moon shaped stone with concentric circles of different designed which guards the entrance to all temples and also serves as a step. Even modern temples have moonstones, of concrete.

Every temple had its guardstones and you will see many in Sri Lanka. The finest examples are to be found at **Ratnaprasada**, a little further north-west. These 8th-century guardstones illustrate a cobra king and are considered to be one of the most refined of designs.

Anuradhapura has three great tanks, as well as many smaller ones. Some of them have fallen into disuse or even been filled in against the threat of malaria. Malaria, as well as the invading Tamils, has been blamed for the total disappearance of the population of Anuradhapura during the centuries when the jungle strangled the sacred city. The 100,000 or so people who live around Anuradhapura today are squatters who moved in when the British started excavating the city in the late 1890s. The big tanks are the **Nuwarawewa** which covers about 1,214.6 hectares (3,000 acres), the much smaller **Tissawewa**, covering about 162 hectares (400 acres), and the northern tank, the **Bassawak Kulama** which is considered to be one of the oldest tanks, dating from about the 4th century BC.

Just 11 km (seven miles) north-east out of Anuradhapura is **Mihintale** a place not only strikingly beautiful but deeply significant to Buddhists. Mihintale is located on top of a rocky mountain.

From the base of Mihintale to the summit is a stairway of 1,840 big granite steps. The first 350 steps are gentle and broad. After this steep narrow stairway leads up to the **Kantaka Cetiya Dagaba,** standing some 12 m (39 ft) high, but probably more than 30 m (98.4 ft) high at one time. It was built before 60 BC but still has some very fine carvings. Around the Dagaba are a number of rock cells, used by hermit monks for their meditations.

Near the middle of the last flight of steps is the **Bhojana Salava** or refectory of the priests. Then a narrow path leads to the **Nagfa Pokuna,** a four-metre bathing pool made from solid rock and lorded over by the carving of a five-headed cobra.

A higher dagaba known as the **Maha Seya** has been recently excavated and is said to contain the real relics of Mahinda.

The Mihintale towers above the lush verdure of the surrounding countryside and commands an excellent view of the other ancient monuments.

The magnificently carved statue of the Reclining Buddha in the Gal Vihara.

Once you are at ground level again, look around at the ruins surrounding the base. This was once a hospital. There is a shallow rock bed cut into the shape of a human figure in which the patient would have lain to have an oil bath. This method of treatment is still used by the ayurvedic or natural healers.

The Aukuna Buddha: Not very far from Anuradhapura is the towering **Buddha of Aukuna**. It is situated along the road that borders the large Kalawewa tank. On your way to the Buddha, you will notice the artificial canal, called the **Yoda Ela**.It is about 12 m (39 ft) wide and about 86 km (53 miles) long and is remarkable as a feat of engineering.

It is a bouncy ride along the road to the Aukuna Buddha, past scrub and coconut plantations. There are few sights more impressive than this magnificent statue, towering about 12 m (39 ft) from its base. Aukuna means "sun-eating" and the best time to see it is at dawn, when the light hits the Buddha's face. The statue is superb, looking much taller than its measured height. Although carved from the rock, it stands out form it. Its face is strong and benign, with the serenity of the early sculpture of Sri Lanka. The right hand is raised in blessing and the robes seem to flow in a way that endows the huge statue with a curious levity. The Buddha stands on a separate plinth in the shape of a lotus and, although visitors view it from the rock opposite, pilgrims go down to its feet to lay their offerings of flowers.

The age of the statue is a matter of controversy and, oddly enough, for all its eighty tons of stone, little is known of its origins.

Approaching the Aukuna Buddha from its base, you will see how gifted the sculptors were. They have even allowed for the foreshortening effect of ground-level perspective. It is a perfect piece of work.

Yapahuwa

While you are driving south from Anuradhapura, it is worth continuing on down to **Maho**, where the Trincomalee-Colombo railway splits off from the Colombo-Jaffna railway. It is not for Maho itself you should stop, but for **Yapahuwa**, a second (and much smaller) rock fortress to Sigiriya.

Yapahuwa means beautiful hill. On the run from invading Tamils, the Singhalese king, Bhuveneka Bahu I, moved his capital there between 1272 and 1284. Before that, Yapahuwa had long been the refuge of Buddhist hermits. Raven-Hart describes it enthusiastically as "like nowhere else in Ceylon: nowhere is there such a riot of sculpture, such a revelry of stone-frozen movement."

Polonnaruwa

Many visitors respond far more to Polonnaruwa than they do to Anuradhapura. That is because Anuradhapura is less accessible to the casual visitor. It takes time, extensive reading and a very good guide to begin to unfold the mysteries and delights of the sacred city. On the other hand, it is easy to see what remains of Polonnaruwa; many of the buildings that still stand are in reasonably good repair and the visitor can readily appreciate their glory. However, Polonnaruwa lacks the atmosphere and grandeur of Anuradhapura.

Polonnaruwa was the phoenix which rose briefly from the ashes of Anuradhapura. It was used as a royal residence by the kings of Anuradhapura in the 8th, 9th and 10th centuries. In the 11th century, the ancient kingdom of Anuradhapura fell to the invading Tamil kings, the Cholas. However, it was the Singhalese King Vijayabahu I (1056-1111) who established himself at Polonnaruwa after he defeated the Cholas in battle. The city flourished further under his successors, Parakrama Bahu I and Nissanka Malla. This mixed Tamil and Singhalese influence gives Polonnaruwa its interesting blend of South Indian and Singhalese architecture which cannot be found elsewhere in Sri Lanka.

Under the rule of Nissanka Malla, the city's glory began to fade. This was due to lack of money for carrying out the king's ambitious projects and threats of invasion from the Tamils.

A good way to start your visit to Polonnaruwa is to have a meal at the Rest House where some of the best curries in Sri Lanka are served at a modest cost. The most commonly offered fish in the countryside is the tank fish but this has a flat, muddy flavor. You would do better to order river fish, which is usually easily available and more tasty. Queen Elizabeth II of England graced this Rest House with her royal presence in 1954. Moreover, she had lunch there. The Rest House is a good spot from which to enjoy the spectacular sunset while drinking cold beer.

Sights of Polonnaruwa

The remains of the ancient city are a short walk from the Rest House. The first ruins you are likely to come upon are those of the **King's Council Chamber** and other royal citadel ruins. This complex was once enclosed by ramparts four leagues long and seven leagues wide and must have been very imposing in its original state.

Nearby, in the same group, is the **Audience Hall**. Take a close look at the frieze of elephants round its base, each one individually crafted, as is usual in the best examples of Singhalese buildings. This building has been nicknamed "The Pavilion of Elephants".

The **Kumara Pokuna**, Prince's Bathing Pool, is to be found in the south-east corner. This handsome little pool, now dried out, was rediscovered in 1935.

Past the north gate of the citadel is the **Sita Devala 2**. Constructed in the 11th century, it is the oldest building in Polonnaruwa, with a purely South Indian style of architecture and a Hindu shrine. The inscriptions in Tamil indicate the date it was built – during the Chola occupation of the city.

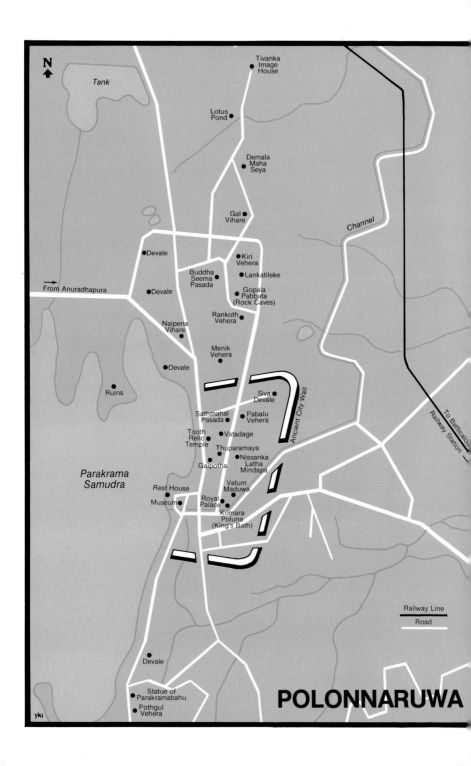

POLONNARUWA

The **Thuperama** is an oblong brick image house, also strongly influenced by Hindu architecture. It is, however, a Buddhist shrine with several Buddha images. While the shrine itself dates back to the 12th century, it is thought that the statues originated in the 8th century. The vaulted roof of the building is still intact.

Like the Thuperama of Anuradhapura, the Vatadage is another fine example of a circular relic house, with an elegance and beauty not usually found even among the ancient buildings of Sri Lanka. The relic house stands by the entrance to the quadrangle. The stone pillars in the outer circle are 18 m (59 ft) in diameter and faced by a screen wall patterned with four-petalled flowers. The moonstone at the north entrance is thought to be the finest in Polonnaruwa, although now it is slightly worn.

Rankot Vihara is the biggest dagaba in Polonnaruwa. It was built by Nissanka Malla in obvious imitation of those to be seen at Anuradhapura. It measures some 165 m (541 ft) in girth and stands some 54 m (177 ft) high. The **Lankatileke** (the Ornament of Ceylon) is the largest shrine in the area, measuring 51 by 19 m (167 by 62 ft) . This is one of the most striking examples of Buddhist art to be found in Sri Lanka.

The vaulted roof has long since collapsed. The builders in Polonnaruwa did not really master the art of the arch: they built brickwork until it met in the center, but the actual arch is slightly beyond them. This is why most arch-like roofs constructed here have collapsed. In the 12th century, the Lankatileke must have been one of the marvels of Asia. Now alas, the great standing Buddha is headless. But the statue is still considered sacred and offerings of flowers are still to be found at the Buddha's feet.

Up the road a little way brings the visitor to what is for most people the most impressive part of Polonnaruwa – the extraordinary statues of the **Gal Vihara**. These must surely mark the peak period of sculpture in Sri Lanka and it is worth taking the time just to sit and stare at these statues. Banish the guides – there is so much disagreement about what the figures represent that your own imagination cannot possibly be far away from whatever the truth might be – and meditate upon what you see.

The standing Buddha is almost seven meters (23 ft) tall and has a sorrowful expression, while the reclining Buddha is almost 14 m (46 ft) long. There is a fine seated Buddha meditating in the lotus position and a smaller similar image of the same. The most impressive of the figures is the reclining Buddha. Experts are not agreed whether the statue shows the Buddha sleeping, meditating or entering the state of "utter passing away" (Mahaparinirvana). Observe in the reclining figure how the contours of the body and the couch touch, even to the dip in the pillow beneath the Buddha's head. Observe, too, the serenity and strength of the figure, how the texture and colors of the rock have all been incorporated into the carving. It is not surprising that it is considered the zenith of Sri Lanka's early sculpture.

The **Lotus Bath** is another of Nissanka Malla's works built, as the name suggests, in the shape of a lotus. There are five concentric rings of petals and you can step down in to each one and into the empty pool.

The **Tivanka Image House** ends the northern road. It is the largest of the brick-built shrines of Polonnaruwa. within the image house is an unusual Buddha statue, standing in the "thrice-bent" pose, hence the name Tivanka. This is a pose more usual to female statues and seldom found in a Buddha statue.

Like Anuradhapura, the ancient city of Polonnaruwa became overgrown by the jungle. Even in the 1880s a visitor described the whole area as being full of wild pigs, and with the tracks of elephants everywhere. Most of what you see today is what the Archaeological Department has reclaimed from the jungle over the past 50 years.

Where to Stay

If you decide to stay in Polonnaruwa, then the Rest House is the obvious place to choose. It is modestly priced, has pleasant rooms, and is in the heart of the city. There is a new town of Polonnaruwa in which you could find home-stay accommodation if you wanted.

If you have the time and inclination, you might like to include a visit to **Medirigiriya**, some 24 km (15 miles) north of Polonnaruwa along a reasonably good (in fair weather) road. There is a building there which is something like the Vatadage but finer. Raven-Hart comments that "it is the most perfect ancient monument in Ceylon". It has three concentric circles of octagonal monolithic pillars with good capitals surrounding an early dagaba.

Sigiriya

Of all the ancient places of Sri Lanka which can be visited today. Sigiriya is still the most impressive, even though so little of its original grandeur remains. It must once have been astounding – a mighty fortress of rock crowned with a great palace. Now only the foundations remain. It was extraordinary in its time, with a strange and bloody history behind it. It is still extraordinary now.

The countryside surrounding Sigiriya is gently hilly and lushly green. It is very rural, the roads awash with waves of butterflies. In this country quiet, there is no preparation at all for the startling eruption of rock which rises straight upwards in a column of stone. The pillar of gneiss rock soars straight up through the jungle which surrounds it. It was right on the top of this towering column that Kasyapa, the father-killer, built his fortress.

The Chulavamsa – the Lesser Chronicle, written by the orthodox Buddhist monks of the king's orders – has nothing good to say about

Kasyapa, which perhaps is not surprising. His father was King Dhuta Sena and the rightful heir to the throne was Kasyapa's brother, Moggallana. Kasyapa was determined to seize power for himself. In view of his later behavior, it might be fair to assume that he was more than a little mad. It is certainly obvious that he felt very little filial gratitude. He imprisoned his father the king, and demanded from him the treasures which were supposed to have gone to his brother, the heir to the throne. Meanwhile, his brother Moggallana wisely made off to India. Legend says that Kasyapa stripped his father naked, chained him up in a cell and then walled him up to die. Then perhaps fearing the reaction of the citizens of the sacred city of Anuradhapura, Kasyapa made off to the impregnable rock of Sigiriya to make himself a fortress at its summit. He took with him an engineer who obviously shared his mad genius and who designed and built a palace for the parricide. That was in 477 AD.

Madman and murderer though he may have been, Kasyapa nevertheless had a vision that worked. Even today it would be an awesome task for anyone even to contemplate building something atop the Sigiriya rock. It is starkly straight and, one would think, technically formidable. Even more incredible is that all the work was done over a period of 18 years.

Sigiriya is more widely known for its **rock-face paintings**. Although this reputation is justified, people are often in so much of a hurry to get up to them that they fail to appreciate the sheer mastery of the whole project. People puff and pant up to the narrow wall of paintings and do not pause to look around sufficiently at the structures on the rock nor at the ramparts and moats surrounding the base below.

The paintings are to be found in a sheltered dip in the rock face on the western side. The ascent to the paintings is an adventure in itself, though a fairly safe one for all but the physically disabled and those who suffer from a fear of heights. Never mind, though, for the steep and sweaty climb will give you a tremendous sense of achievement and virtue when you actually reach the paintings. You will have to make you way across the wavelike surface of the rock itself, with small footholds cut into it and an iron handrail nearby with sinister bends in it every now and then, as if someone had . . .

If you do not suffer from vertigo, then keep stopping as you climb, to take in the view below you. If may not be the most beautiful in Sri Lanka, but it must be the widest.

Once you finally reach the pictures, you may feel a slight sense of anticlimax. One sees them reproduced so often, and so well, that it is slightly disappointing to find that there are only 18 paintings, and the majority of them are damaged. These are all that is left of the 500 or so portraits of lovely maidens with their warmly sensitive faces and their full young breasts.

No one knows who or what they are. There are various suggestions – that they are goddesses and heavenly spirits. They are perhaps more likely to be the dancing girls and court women sadly missed by the soldiers guarding Kasyapa in his mad flight from his own evil deeds. Whoever they are, these women have had their admirers over many centuries. We know this from the so-called mirror wall on the next level above the paintings. On the surface of this wall, men and women have recorded their impressions of the maidens and the great scholar Professor Paranavitana has recorded their scribblings in two massive volumes published as *The Sigiriya Graffiti*. The "mirror" part of the name is very fanciful since the wall has only a slight sheen, created by application of a mixture of eggs, honey and limestone powder.

The ascent to the summit itself, which comes after the paintings, is even more exciting. A delicate wrought-iron staircase spirals tremblingly up the wall, supplemented by a footpath of tiny toeholds. About 500 visitors a day make the climb up to where the extraordinary palace of Sigirya was erected. On the way, you pass between two giant paws like those of the sphinx. They are all that remain of a huge image of a lion, made of brick and stucco, which used to peer out towards the north, from where Kasyapa thought his brother would come to avenge their father's murder. It was from this mighty lion that the name Sigiriya – the lion rock – came.

The Palace Ruins

The ruins of the palace on the summit cover some 1.6 hectares (4 acres). It used to have 128 rooms, including some which must have been virtually hanging over the edge of the rock. It was no mere utilitarian fortress hangout though. It had gardens, bathing pool, cisterns, music rooms, audience halls – everything a real palace of the time might need.

You will notice a metal cage on the flat courtyard down by the lion's paws. Some deadly hornets live in the rocks. A few years ago, a woman fainted in the heat and her husband called for help. Unfortunately, the deadly insects took exception to his voice and both were badly stung. That is why there is a metal mesh cage there. If by any chance you see the hornets, get in. Also, keep your voice down, though it is merely a precaution.

As Kasyapa had dreaded, Moggallana did indeed come to avenge his father and Kasyapa stabbed himself to death, thus ending the 18-year occupation of the fortress in the sky.

Where to Stay

There are several choices of accommodation near Sigiriya. There is the luxury **Sigiriya Village Hotel**. It is not cheap to stay there, but it is

Ascending the rock fortress oat Sigiriya.

one of the best new hotels you are likely to come across in Sri Lanka. It is a splendid piece of design, with accommodation laid out in bungalows, each room individually decorated, each section of units built around a theme. It is heartening to find a hotel where such trouble has been taken to ensure high standards. On the cheaper side, there is the **Sigiriya Rest House**. And nearby there is the **Upsara National Holiday Resort**, a pleasant camping ground with wooden huts and even a couple of treetop cabins. These are very cheap and bedding and food are provided by the camp officials for a modest fee. It appears to be sadly under-used.

From Sigiriya you can take a picturesque drive to **Trincomalee**. The countryside is made up of many little lanes, woolly with trees and filled with a continuous buzzing chorus from the invisible small beetles called *raiyar*.

Do take a stop at the **Kantilai Guest House**, either for lunch or tea, or overnight. The house overlooks the Kantila Lake which is surrounded by trees and therefore by birds. At the southern end of the lake there are a series of small lagoons that form a natural sanctuary for water-birds.

Dambulla Caves

You can visit the Dambulla Caves before or after going to Sigiriya, as they are only a few miles down the road.

History tells us that these caves sheltered the fleeing King Vattagamini Abhaya, back in the first century BC. He had been the ruling king of Anuradhapura, but the sacred city was constantly endangered by repeated invasions by the Tamils of South India. It had become too rich and too famous for its own good and the Singhalese were no match for the fierce Tamil warriors. Poor Vattagamini left his capital 64 km (40 miles) behind him and made off with his family, seeking safety in the depths of the caves, already known as a Buddhist shrine.

One approaches the caves by turning off the road and walking up a wavelike rock which seems to have rippled slowly down from some mythical volcano long since disappeared. It is a 105-m (345-ft) climb up to the caves and the climb is steep. It is a good idea to set out early in the day to avoid the heat and glare. As the caves are a place of pilgrimage, there are cripples there to beg from the pilgrims who gain religious merit by the donation of alms. Although you might get fed up with them, just remember that life is grim for the crippled in Sri Lanka and that you can well afford some coins.

You will fortunately have good reason to stop every few yards, as the views are stunning all the way along the path. This will give you breathing space while you look out over the panoramic vista of countryside. For non-Buddhists this is full recompense for the arduous ascent.

Once at the caves, head straight for the most distant one, shaking off would-be guides on the way. These guides are a real pest at Dambulla.

Not only are they ill-informed, but they are noisy, aggressive and leave you little change to appreciate any serenity the caves might offer. They are obsessed by figures – monetary, heights and lengths. If there is anything you want to know, there are some friendly monks in the small monastery at the caves.

Whatever work King Vattagamini Abhaya commissioned for the caves, as well as the later additions of King Nissanka Malla (who had the interior of the temple gilded), nothing now remains. The work you see is of comparatively recent origin, not even 100 years old. There are said to be some copies of more ancient works among the paintings and statues.

While it may not be fair to judge the caves by the quality of their artwork, any more than we judge Christian churches by their statuary, the greatest attraction of Dambulla for those of other faiths is nevertheless likely to be the superb views around it.

There is a Rest House at Dambulla, with friendly management, clean, good-sized rooms, and reasonable but not exceptional food. They have the strange habit of asking you if you like meat or fish, and then suddenly producing these things cooked allegedly Western-style on the grounds that you have ordered them. Be sure that you specify clearly what you want to eat. Their Sri Lankan food is much better than their Western food, but specify that you do want spices or you'll get few. It is nevertheless a pleasant place to stay and is modestly priced.

The Hill Country

The heart of Sri Lanka is beautiful hill country. The area is favored by Sri Lankans because it is cool and restorative after the sticky humidity of the coast and plains. Rolling green hills, deep valleys falling hundreds of metres and some of the highest waterfalls in the world form a backdrop at once luxuriant and refreshing. The tea plantations standing crew-cut across the hilltops, the misty mornings, and the beautiful, unspoiled walks compound the contrast. Then, too, there is the slightly fossilized town of Nuwara Eliya, once the summer retreat of the British and still regarded as fashionable among the Sri Lankans, and the capital of Kandy with its slight air of frivolity and its rococo architecture. The charisma is complete.

A number of tourists have reported that they did not enjoy the hills, that they left as soon as they reasonably could. In almost every case this seemed to be because they had not gone there prepared for the weather.

After you have become accustomed to the temperature of the seaside resorts and the plains, you will find it cold in the hills unless you go well equipped with warm clothing. You need a sweater, a windcheater (preferably one that will fold up very small), warm socks and proper shoes and possibly an umbrella (although you can buy one cheaply enough in the hilltowns). You also need to make sure that your accommodation has extra heating in the form of electric fires, log fires or central heating. Do not take accommodation in a place which does not undertake to supply extra heat, and check the blankets too. If there aren't enough, demand more. If they won't give extra blankets, don't stay there. Once you have taken care of your creature comforts, you will find that you will thoroughly enjoy all the delights that the hills can offer. There are many.

The Hill Country Tour

There are many ways to take to the hills. A glance at the map of Sri Lanka will help you to select which places suit any one itinerary. the important thing is to allow yourself enough time to see places and to absorb them. Most people make the mistake of spending one day in the hills, half a day in Kandy, and so on. They leave Sri Lanka knowing little of what they have seen and understanding nothing of its lifestyles or people.

You can approach the hills from Hambantota on the southern coast, or from Colombo. It is easy to vary your route. Some travelers may prefer to start at some of the less developed places in the hills and finish at Kandy. Kandy has so much to offer that it might make other places pall. But it is a city. For those who like the country life of the hills, then places like Haputale, Ella, Horton Plains and other small towns are better choices. Haputale, Nuwara Eliya and Ella make good centers from which to take day trips. for nostalgia buffs, it has to be Nuwara Eliya, a leftover from the grand old days of British colonial rule.

A suggested route is to start from Kandy, the real center of Singhalese culture, then proceed to Nuwara Eliya via Gampola, Hatton, Nanu Oya and the many tea gardens, with side trips to Horton Plains and Mount Pedro; Welimada and Bandarawela with its beautiful mountain scenery and forest views; Haputale, with the English mansion of Adisham, the five-provinces view and good walks; Badulla, known for the Dunhinda Falls, the sixth highest in the world; Ella with the Ella Gap View, the best in Sri Lanka; then south to Hambantota via Wellawaya to see Rawana Falls, Diyaluma Falls and the giant standing Buddha of Buduruvagala.

Kandy

Kandy has an atmosphere of its own. It certainly cannot be appreciated in a day. Situated about 465 m (1,526 ft) above sea level, it curves up and down the hills which cluster round a man-made lake. The cities of Sri Lanka are not on the whole attractive but Kandy compares favorably with other beautiful cities. Like Srinigar in Kashmir, Bhadgaon in Nepal and Macau in the south China Sea, Kandy is delightful just to look at. Houses and villas are situated up and down the hillsides above the lake, peering from their fringe of trees. The surrounding countryside

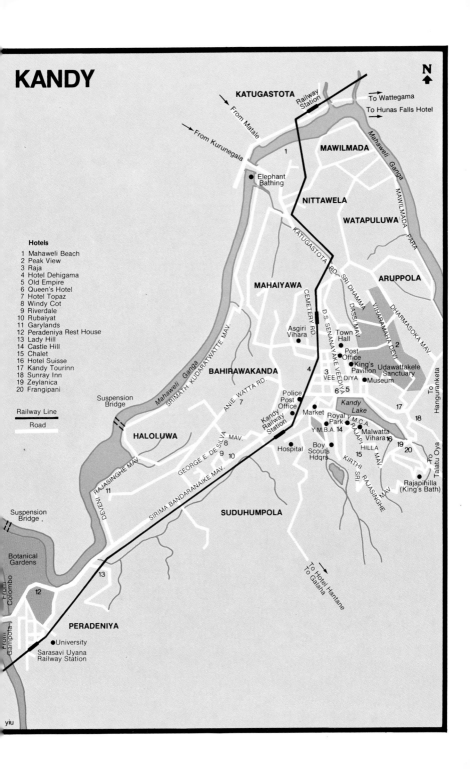

KANDY

N

KATUGASTOTA

Railway Station

To Wattegama

To Hunas Falls Hotel

From Matale

From Kurunegala

MAWILMADA

Elephant Bathing

NITTAWELA

WATAPULUWA

ARUPPOLA

MAHAIYAWA

Asgiri Vihara

Town Hall

Post Office

King's Pavilion

Udawattakele Sanctuary

Museum

BAHIRAWAKANDA

Police Post Office

Kandy Railway Station

Market

Royal Park

Kandy Lake

Y.M.C.A.

Y.M.B.A.

Malwatta Vihara

HALOLUWA

Hospital

Boy Scouts Hdqrs

Rajapihilla (King's Bath)

Suspension Bridge

SUDUHUMPOLA

To Hotel Hantane

To Galaha

Suspension Bridge

Botanical Gardens

From Colombo

From Gampola

PERADENIYA

University

Sarasavi Uyana Railway Station

Hotels

1. Mahaweli Beach
2. Peak View
3. Raja
4. Hotel Dehigama
5. Old Empire
6. Queen's Hotel
7. Hotel Topaz
8. Windy Cot
9. Riverdale
10. Rubaiyat
11. Garylands
12. Peradeniya Rest House
13. Lady Hill
14. Castle Hill
15. Chalet
16. Hotel Suisse
17. Kandy Tourinn
18. Sunray Inn
19. Zeylanica
20. Frangipani

Railway Line

Road

yiu

is picture-pretty, with paddy fields, palm trees, water birds, and lovely nests of village houses, all encompassed within the wide sweep of the Mahaveli River, Sri Lanka's largest. Kandy is best seen at dawn and at dusk, so ensure you get up early one morning to attend the morning Puja at the Temple of the Tooth and to watch the city come to life.

The Kandyan kings used to be splendidly rich but as time went by they squandered their resources with royal abandon. However, they painted, decorated, improved and built almost everywhere, leaving their mark for future generations. Kandy-striped must surely have originated here as you will appreciate when you see the richness of the boldly painted pink buildings with their extravagant, frothy architecture. There is altogether a charming flamboyance to Kandy. You need a week there, a month even.

Where to Stay

Choose your temporary home with care. The Queen's Hotel is the oldest hotel in Sri Lanka, dating back to 1841, and it is the most frequented by foreign visitors. The Oberoi group of hotels has recently taken over its management and is upgrading its standards. The curry restaurant is splendid.

Kandy has many excellent home-stay places. The Rambukwella Walauwa, Yatiwala, near the Katugastota Elephant Bath is inexpensive, the food is wonderful and the house and garden beautiful. There are other places like this too. Ask around and go and see.

A word of warning: don't go to an alleged spice garden and beware of the Elephant Bath. Spices grow wild around these hills and you can see them everywhere. A spice garden is an enterprising little tourist trap – a small patch of garden where someone has grown some spices which have been bought at the market in Kandy. If you want to buy spices, go where Sri Lankans go – down to the market. You will still be slightly overcharged but not nearly so much.

The elephants you see at the Elephant Bath being bathed by their mahouts are working elephants hired out by the mahouts for 100 rupees a day to be photographed by tourists for 50 rupees per picture. Don't go there. The mahouts can be aggressive and unpleasant. There are other places where you can photograph elephants. If you are returning to Colombo, you will have a chance to visit the Elephant Orphanage at Kegalle where you may look at the elephants and take all the pictures you want. For further information please contact: Department of National Zoological Gardens, tel: 71-2751/3, 71-4542.

Peradeniya Botanical Garden

About five kilometers (three miles) outside Kandy is the Peradeniya Botanical Garden which offers a unique chance to see Sri Lanka's treasury of plants. More than 25 per cent of the world's plant life is represented somewhere in Sri Lanka, and a visit to the botanical garden is a good way of seeing them. There is a modest entrance fee and a cheap brochure available. It gives valuable background information and is a good guide to what you will find inside the garden.

Before Kandy became a royal capital, Peradeniya was the site of a royal residence and palace garden during the reign of King Kirti Sri Raja Shinha (1747-82). The botanical garden was opened in 1821, six years after the Kandyan kings surrendered their kingdom to the British.

This was no random act of kindness by the new British masters. It was part of the colonial habit to set up such garden in various outposts of the Empire. They supplied not only important scientific knowledge but also additional revenue. When the garden was set up at Peradeniya the officials who ran it were warned to make sure it produced a profit. It took a while to find a suitable site, but the first superintendent managed to buy up a tract of land along the curve of the Mahaveli River. The Peradeniya garden was thus well watered, and the climate was ideal at a steady 22 °C (72 °F). The golden age of the garden began in 1848, when Henry Kendrick Thwaites was appointed Director. The 27-year-old director was a man of vision. He planted tea bushes and cinchona trees from which the anti-malarial drug, quinine, was manufactured. When the coffee blight wiped out many plantations, Thwaites was able to supply the plantations of affected coffee-growers with new tea and cinchona saplings, from which considerable revenue was generated for the British colonial government.

The best times to visit the gardens are from 8 am to 10 am, and when the heat of the day is over, from 4 pm to 6 pm. What makes Peradeniya delightful is its spaciousness, the variety of its plants and groves and the number of little pathways. Here you can wander at will and enjoy yourself in a leisurely way. There are no hawkers trying to sell you anything, no man, woman or child pestering you for money.

Peradeniya has a spice garden, a medicinal herb garden (with an unmarked cocaine plant if you can find it), a fern garden, and aromatic grasses. In the bamboo grove is the giant bamboo, the tallest plant in the world, which grows at the rate of 0.6 m (2 ft) a day. There are orchid houses, flower beds and flowering shrubs and a cannonball tree with its giant fruit hanging from the trunk.

The garden is also a display center for rubber trees. There is an old story that the rubber trees were smuggled out of Brazil, but in fact they were given as a legitimate gift to a British official who took them to Kew Gardens in London and then sent some seedlings to Peradeniya. The early experiments led to the germination of the seeds and Sri Lanka's rubber industry was launched.

Temple of the Tooth

Once you have seen the Peradeniya Gardens, Kandy's next main attraction is the Temple of the Tooth (Dalada Maligawa). This 16th

The Temple of the Tooth in Kandy.

century shrine houses a tooth of the Buddha. Before coming to rest here, the Tooth relic rested in Anuradhapura in the 4th century and was moved several times after that, due to the constant upheavals and invasions which troubled Sri Lanka during the ensuing centuries. The tooth was said to have been snatched from the flamed of the Buddha's funeral pyre in 543 BC.

Experts who have actually seen the tooth claim that the size is nothing like that of a human tooth. Buddhists counter by saying that what they have seen is only the outer enclosure of the tooth.

Whatever the real story, there is no doubt that Buddhists all over Sri Lanka venerate the Tooth Relic in the shrine in Kandy. The temple you see today is not the first one built on the site to house the relic. The first was a three-story building later destroyed by the Portuguese. It was replaced by a two-story structure, which was repaired by King Kirti Sri Raja Sinha.

Daily rituals are enacted in the Temple to venerate the relic. The first of the ceremonies starts before 6 am. You can enter the actual shrine room upstairs, where the jeweled relic case is on show. There are some tourists who get up early in the morning to watch the ceremonies, as the dawn rite is the most impressive of all, but the majority of the visitors who go to the temple are religious pilgrims requesting special favors or giving thanks for blessings received.

Replica of casket of the Golden Tooth, Kandy.

The Kandy Asala Perahera

Once a year, the replica of the Tooth Relic casket is paraded through the town of Kandy in the astonishing ritual of the Perahera. The Kandy Perahera is both a religious ritual and a folk festival, unparalleled in color and spectacle. Elephants with glorious jeweled canopies, Kandyan drummers, dancers and priests participate in a procession that is one of the most spectacular in Asia. The festival is held in the lunar month of Asala, around July or August, and lasts for ten days and nights.

Unfortunately the Perahera is not free from exploitation. Hotels put up their prices to unbelievable heights and thieves and pickpockets are out in force.

By the way, if you are interested in Kandyan dance and drumming, you don't have to wait for the Perahera. There are performances in most of the bigger hotels in Kandy which are reasonably good.

Other Temples

Two of the most famous temples in Kandy, and the two most influential in Sri Lanka, are the Malwatte and Asgiriya temples. The Asgiriya is the seat of the other arch abbot of the Siamese sect in Kandy and lies up the hill behind the mosque. The temples divide into old (18th century) and new (19th century). The old temple has a good altar piece and some fine 19th-century carved doorways. In the new temple there is an interesting rock carving of a Buddha.

Museums

There are two museums in Kandy – the National Museum and the Archaeological Museum. The National is housed in what used to be the quarters of the royal concubines, while the Archaeological is all that remains of the royal palace of the former kings of Kandy. Both have many interesting exhibits which illustrate the richness and varied history of the Kandyan kingdom. The National Museum is open from 9 am to 5 pm, except on Fridays and Saturdays. The Archaeological Museum is open from 8 am until 4 pm, except on Tuesdays.

Also in the vicinity of the Tooth Temple is the Audience Hall, an authentic Kandyan building. It was in this hall that the last king of Kandy, Sri Wickrama Rajasinha, ceded the territories of his kingdom to the British.

Shopping

There are two places in Kandy recommended for shopping. One is the thriving market in the middle of town, near the buses. This is a large, sprawling building of several storys. There are also stalls round the outside. It is one of the most attractive markets you are likely to come across in Sri Lanka. you can buy spices here, but hard bargaining is necessary.

The second shopping place is the Kandyan Art Association and Government Handicrafts Shop (Laksala) where you can buy local crafts and even see them being made. Kandy was always rich in craftsmanship, which largely came under the patronage of the kings.

Kandy is the center of many of Sri Lanka's crafts, but the ones that are actually produced here are very touristy. Designs are endlessly reproduced. Few craftsmen seem to be producing new and good original work. Much of the stuff is garish and the brass work tends to be very thin. Still, you will get fair prices at the Laksala stores, which is not the case in the private shops in Kandy where prices are outrageously high.

Excursions from Kandy

Hunasgiriya Falls

One of the delights of Kandy is the number of trips you can take into the surrounding countryside. Among the most spectacular is the ride out to the Hunasgiriya Falls along a winding mountain road, with wide vistas of the blue misty hills and valleys below. Spices grow wild, and you will see at least eight or nine kinds of spices. Look out for the pepper vines twisting up tree trunks and growing pods in shiny green clusters, and cinnamon bushes with dark green leaves.

The falls are manifestly impressive. Just beside the falls is the Hunas Falls Hotel where you can stop for light refreshments.

Western Shrines

About 16 km (10 miles) from Kandy, on the Kadugannuwa-Peradeniya Road, is a small complex of temples known as the Western Shrines. these are Gadaladeniya, Lankatilleke and Embekke. The Gadaladeniya is built of somber grey stone and stands on rock. Many consider it to be the most beautifully situated temple in Sri Lanka. It is attractively domed and features an interesting porch.

The next shrine along the road leading south is Lankatillcke. It is a striking building, more reminiscent of a Norwegian church made in sugar icing than a Buddhist shrine. The roof is of comparatively recent origin, only about 100 years old. The building within is the typical plain oblong to be found throughout Singhalese architecture. Raven-Hart surmises that small shrines raised to various gods became so frequently visited by worshipers that chapel-like additions were made to the original simple building. What the visitor sees today is one inner Buddhist shrine with six dewalas (shrines) to other gods. The frescoes inside are good and are probably 300 years old.

Of the three shrines, Embekke is the most attractive, although the simplest. You approach it through a village where the people tend not to bother visitors (unlike villages close to other shrines where demands for money are incessant). There is a thriving local craft in silver and brass work which you might be politely asked to look at but no one minds very much if you don't buy anything.

Delgadoruwa, a few kilometers from Kandy along the Teldeniya Road, is famous for its recently restored frescoes illustrating Tales from the Jataka. These paintings form a valuable record of daily life in Kandy in the late 18th century and are considered the best of their kind.

Medawela, also a few kilometers from Kandy, is an 18th-century temple, simple and rustic in design.

Dodanwela is a 14th-century temple and its main point of historic interest is that King Raja Sinha of Kandy gave his crown and sword as an offering in this temple after he defeated the Portuguese in battle. The crown and sword are still preserved in the temple.

Other Sights

At the Royal Palace Park overlooking the lake you will find a cannon donated by Lord Louis Mountbatten, who had his wartime headquarters at the Peradeniya Gardens during World War II. The cannon was captured from the Japanese in Burma. On the other side of the lake is the Udawattakele Sanctuary, with its birds, monkeys and wildlife. It is a beautiful and peaceful place to take a walk, but in the company of other people. There have bccn a few robberies here, so reasonable care should

be taken. Walk up towards the summit of the hills, around the lake at sundown for a wonderful twilight view of the city and a chance to enjoy the sunset.

Kegalle

Kegalle is a small village on the Kandy to Colombo road. Its main point of interest is the nearby Elephant Orphanage.

Baby elephants may be abandoned for a number of reasons: the mother has been killed by poachers or has died, or the babies have been rejected by their mothers or left behind by the herd. Concerned about the plight of elephants abandoned in the national parks, the Wildlife Conservation Department set up a sanctuary where they could be cared for.

The youngest to come to the sanctuary have been a couple of months old; younger than that they die very quickly. Once rescued, they are kept with the other elephants and fed milk several times a day in vast quantities. As soon as they show an interest, they can start eating vegetarian, their favorite kind being the young kitul palm. An elephant can tuck away a palm tree a day, so they need considerable ground for grazing. The orphanage makes an ideal stopping place for a picnic.

Scenic Route

When driving from Kandy to Nuwara Eliya, take the longer but more scenic route, passing Geli Oya, Gampola, Ginigathena, Norton Bridge, Kotagala, Hatton, Lindula and Nanu Oya, which takes you through breathtaking landscapes of paddy fields and palms, small villages and hillsides where people work the fields with buffaloes, small children fish and friendly people wave at you. Beyond this, the hills become wilder and more woolly with bushes and trees, eventually leading to the valleys and slopes of tea. Then there comes an entire valley of rivers flowing silvery through the green, and a valley of some of the most impressive waterfalls you are ever likely to see, tumbling and roaring down, one after the other. You will be stopping constantly either to take photographs or just to drink in the magnificence of the views.

The most noticeable thing about Geli Oya is the extraordinary three-dimensional spider webs strung between the telephone wires. Gampola is an attractive little town lying among rice fields and coconut groves. From what remains today, you would never guess that this was briefly the seat of kings in the 14th century.

The valley leading to Ginigathena is spectacular, one of the most striking in Sri Lanka. Hills give way to mountains. From the valley, you see in the distance the Ramboda Hills, as well as Sri Lanka's highest mountain, Pidurutalagala or Mount Pedro (2,524 m or 8,281 ft high).

(preceding page) Baby elephants being tended at the Elephant Orphanage at Kegalle.

The next stretch of the journey takes you past more cascades and waterfalls. Some of the names remind the visitor that many of the tea plantations were owned by Scottish planters who named their estates, and the countryside around them, after the far-away highlands of Scotland.

Leaving the waterfalls behind, you head for Nuwara Eliya, the heart of the tea country. The Orange Pekoe Ceylon Tea is still one of Sri Lanka's major exports, but the tea industry has suffered rather through lack of investment and loss of skilled personnel.

The first tea plantation, called Loolecondera, was first started in 1867 by James Taylor.

Tea-Growing

Left to nature, the tea bush (a distant relative of the camelia) can grow to a height of nine or even 15 meters (30 or 50 ft). However, for the purpose of picking the leaves, a tea bush is never allowed to grow above three meters (10 ft). There are three elevation heights recognized by the planters and merchants. The first is low-grown, from sea-level to 600 meters (1,969 ft) above sea level. The second is mid-grown, from 600 to 1,200 meters (3,937 ft), and the third is high-grown, above 1,200 meters. The best tea is said to be the high-grown.

The quality of Ceylon tea is determined by the size of the tea leaves. The names for grades are Broken Orange Pekoe, Broken Pekoe, Orange Pekoe and Tippy Tea. Broken Orange Pekoe is the highest grade of Ceylon tea, using the smallest leaf and the unopened bud. Broken Pekoe is picked from the smallest leaf but without the bud. Orange Pekoe comes from larger leaves, and Tippy Tea comes from tips. Raven-Hart says delightfully that Tippy Tea used to go to harems where it was regarded as an aphrodisiac.

Plucking and preparing tea goes on throughout the year, except for a short pruning season. The pickers are all Tamils, who were originally imported from India as cheap labor by the British. They are always referred to as Indian Tamils, to differentiate them from the Sri Lankan Tamils, although in some cases the former have resided in Sir Lanka for many generations. On the whole, they receive low wages and their living conditions are poor.

Once the tea is prepared by the factories, it goes to Colombo for auctioning. Some of it is sent to London for further auctioning. At one time, British tea firms owned and ran all of the estates. Now that the estates have been nationalized, the British tea merchants have a much lower profile.

Most factories are pleased to show visitors around. They do it free, or for a very nominal fee, and do not pressure you into buying anything, though a factory-fresh pound of tea makes an inexpensive and impressive present.

You will see tea gardens all over the hill country, but especially around the towns of Kandy, Nuwara Eliya, Bandarawela, Badulla, Haputale, Diyatalawa and Ratnapura.

Adam's Peak

From Hatton you can proceed to Adam's Peak. This is not the highest mountain in Sri Lanka but it is the most famous. It is sacred to Buddhists, Hindus and Muslims alike. The name also evokes interest from the Christians.

All the early travelers to Sri Lanka mention it. Marco Polo, who was in Sri Lanka around 1293, noted in his travel diary: "In this island there is a very high mountain," and there "the tomb of Adam, our first parent, is supposed to be found."

It is easier to see Adam's Peak from the sea than from the land because it is often hidden in mists. for much of the year these mists and the rain make it hard to climb the Peak. It normally takes about three hours to make the ascent, after a steep climb through mountain paths and forest. The summit is surrounded by a parapet. In the center of a level space is the Sri Pada (the sacred footprint).

King Valagam Bahu (1st century, BC) is said to have discovered this footprint while he was in exile after being driven out by the invading Tamils. He went wandering around the jungle on the Peak and was lured to the top by a deer which vanished. The Buddhists believed this to be the footprint of the lord Buddha.

The pilgrimage season starts in December and runs until the start of the south-west monsoon in April. The Peak is supposed to be clear at this time. Pilgrims arrive by a variety of routes. Most come via Maskeliya, after getting off the train at Hatton. Buses stop near the Dalhousie Tea Factory and the climb begins a mile or so from there. Many pilgrims stop at the Sita Gangula to bathe and put on white clothes of pilgrimage. Steps can be found in the steeper parts of the climb. There are tea-shops and resting places on the way. The last lap is over a very precipitous surface, and ladders, iron railings and chains have been placed there to help the pilgrims.

A longer route, which some take because it gives them more religious merit for their effort, comes from Ratnapura. The ascent starts at the Carney Estate at **Gilimale**, and the climb goes on for some 14 kilometers.

If you make the ascent, you will need a warm sweater and socks and a windcheater, but you will get fairly hot during the climb. Nevertheless, the night on Adam's Peak can be bitterly cold. Dawn is at around 6 am. If you start at 2 am you should get there in time for the sunrise.

Nuwara Eliya

The name Nuwara Eliya means "town of light", but the significance of the name eludes many visitors. It is set in an attractively green

Adam's Peak at sunrise.

countryside, in a little cup of a valley, with a small town center. In the suburbs there are some superb examples of pseudo-English houses. It is quite clear that this was at one time a planter's town and, although it is now a little seedy and run-down, it still has some style.

The two main places of note in Nuwara Eliya are the **Grand Hotel** and the **Hill Club**. The Grand Hotel is impressive from the outside but is overpriced. The Hill Club, on the other hand, is modestly priced, comfortable and the service is excellent. It was founded in 1870s as a planters' club. The portraits of old Victorian Scots still gaze down sternly on the visitors. If you dine there, you are served a five-course meal by white-gloved waiters who keep appearing with dish after dish. this must be the only place in the world where you can have a five-course meal by candlelight without breaking the bank. The meals are very reasonably priced, and you can have lunch or dinner. Lunch can be Sri Lankan food if you want, but dinner is Western – nay, it is British: soup, fish, meat, pudding and cheese. Service is friendly and efficient.

The club has an interesting history. Soon after it was first opened, the coffee blight hit the planters and the club was in danger of folding. However, with the advent of tea, fortunes revived and so, too, did the club. then it was all chaps only and no nonsense. World War I brought more trouble. When the planters returned after the war was over, they found their building in sad repair and decided to raise the money for a new club building. This is the one which stands today. It dates back to the 1920s but looks several hundred years old. Ladies were admitted in the 1930s (but only through a side door).

The club's next crisis came when Sri Lanka became independent. Many members went back to Britain, leaving the membership seriously depleted. Then Sri Lankan nationals became club members and in the early 1970s it was decided that passing visitors could become temporary members, allowing them to stay and eat there. There are some rules to follow. For example, gentlemen must wear ties (one can be hired for a small sum). This does sometimes mean wearing a necktie over a T-shirt, but honor has been satisfied and no one seems to mind.

There are club mementos all over the place – old sporting prints, some very good silver, racing trophies, a reading room, the stuff fish. It is a marvelous piece of nostalgia.

Take your raincoat to Nuwara Eliya because one of the things which makes it so green is its high annual rainfall. It is also cold in the evenings, much more so than in Kandy. It is a good place for exercise, though. There is an 18-hole golf course, a central park with a flower garden which is particularly pleasant in March, and **Gregory's Lake** with its surrounding paths.

Excursions from Nuwara Eliya

From Nuwara Eliya, don't miss a chance to go to **Horton Plain**. The road may be nigh on impassable, and you may have to bounce along in an old jeep at 24 kph (15 mph) but it is worth the trouble just to behold the scenery. There are wooded hills, hedgerows full of tiny wild flowers, and the occasional smooth green meadow.

The whole of Horton Plain is a nature reserve. Unlike the British, the Sri Lankans have no special taste for hunting and shooting, so wild animals and birds abound here. Once it used to be kept exclusively for the planters to live out their leisure time as if they were in Scotland. Indeed the character of the sparse tough plain is very Scottish. It was discovered by a Mr Farr, after whom the **Farr's Inn** is named.

The streams all over Horton Plain are stocked with trout, first introduced by the planters who wanted a good day's fishing when they went up for the holidays. Today, virtually unfished, the waters are teeming with fish. From Farr's Inn to **World's End** is about four kilometers of easy walking, even for the most reluctant hiker. There are many places to stop to appreciate the excellent views all around.

The walk leads through grassy meadows, a stretch of woodland and to a view known as Little World's End. This is best seen from the side of a small hill rising beside the signpost. World's End itself is a smart kilometer or so down a narrow path through the woods. In places the earth here is almost pink-striped from metal deposits in the soil. There are bear-monkeys in the woods and if you walk quietly you will come across them playing in the trees. They are beautiful and harmless. Bird life is abundant. From the very edge of World's End itself one commands a breathtaking view – a 2,000-m (6,562-ft) drop, sheer and sharp to the valley below, as if a giant had pared off the rock.

Although most people say you must go very early, in fact you can – if fortune favors you – get a good view at any time. Hire a jeep and share the cost with others.

Where to Stay

Farr's Inn is the perfect center for those who enjoy walking. Horton Plain, far from being a plain, is actually a plateau at the top of a mountain ridge, and is first-rate for fishing, bird-watching and for those with botanical interests. The Inn, run by the Ceylon Tourist Board, offers rooms and food.

Mount Pedro

Two more excursions worth making out of Nuwara Eliya are to **Mount Pedro**, or Pidurutalagala in Singhalese, and to the **Hakgala Gardens**.

Mount Pedro soars to a height of 2,524 m (8,282 ft) and is the highest point in Sri Lanka. The climb up to the summit starts from Keen Road in the north of Nuwara Eliya, and since Nuwara Eliya is situated at a considerable altitude, the walk to the peak of Mount Pedro is more of a stroll than a climb. It takes two hours to reach the summit along a pleasant single-track path through shady woods. As one approaches the summit, the trees become shorter, clipped back by the wind. There are markers at 2,250 meters and 2,400 meters. A small cairn marks the summit.

Hakgala Gardens

The **Hakgala Gardens** are the second botanical gardens in the hill country (the other one being the Peradeniya Gardens just outside Kandy). Hakgala is about 9 kilometers (6 miles) from Nuwara Eliya. The gardens were started in the 19th century by Sir Clements Markham to grow cinchona saplings for transplanting to the plantations in the hills. Quinine, the anti-malaria drug, is derived from this plant.

Hakgala means "jaw rock", and is said to refer to the rock on which the gardens have been constructed. According to legend, Rama, the hero of the epic *Ramayana*, sent Hanuman the Monkey God to the Himalayans to find a particular medicinal herb. Hanuman set off but forgot what herb it was that Rama wanted so he bit off a whole chunk of the Himalayas and brought it back to Rama – hence the Hakgala Rock.

On the way to Nuwara Eliya there is a small temple called the **Sita Eliya Temple**. It was here (the legends continue) that Rama's wife, Sita, was held captive by the bad King Rawana.

Some travelers have recommended driving through Welimada to Bandarawela which stands at some 1,219 m (4,000 ft) and is the second most popular hill station after Nuwara Eliya. It is certainly warmer and the air is drier. Most rain here comes during the north-east monsoon, from November to January.

Haputale

Haputale is a natural choice for a travel center. It commands a view of undoubted splendor. Looking outwards and downwards from Haputale, the distant blue hills can be seen gradating to misty green valleys below. On the horizon, the imaginative can pick out the outline of the Sleeping Warrior, a series of peaks forming the profile of a man's head lying down. The view strikes the eye with rich colors – red ochres from the soil in the regions below, powerful deep blues, dark greens. It is said that you can see across five provinces from here. Well, maybe.

Haputale itself is not much of a town. One road in, one out, and that's about it. But it is oddly cheerful and bustling in the middle of these peaceful hills, and full of good walks.

Wooden bridges strung over roaring torrents are frequently found throughout Sri Lanka.

Where to Stay

There are plenty of places to stay, from the Monamaya Guest House, much recommended by those who stay there, to the Highcliffe Hotel, also modestly priced and equipped with an excellent book of special excursions, together with detailed maps. This has been compiled by the owner of the hotel and even casual drop-in visitors are welcome to see it.

St Andrew's Church is worth a look. It is exactly like a small Scottish kirk while the countryside land certainly provides the appropriate Caledonian backdrop. In the churchyard lies the Reverend W.S. Senior and on his grave you can read this inscription:

"Here I stand
In spirit as in body once I stood
Long years ago in love with all the land,
This peerless land of bounteous plenitude."

The best view of the five provinces is seen from the first mile of the Dambetanna Road, past the main bus stand in the town.

Adisham

Adisham is a real English country mansion just outside Haputale. Take the Colombo Road and walk past the police station. Three kilometers further on will find a Buddhist temple. About one kilometer on, turn left. The turning point is signposted. The approach to Adisham is through a bird sanctuary.

The mansion was built by Sir Thomas Villier, a tea merchant whose aristocratic connections include the Russels, the Bedfords, and the Clarendons. The house was built in 1931 but it somehow contrives to look about 300 years old and is reminiscent of a Tudor mansion. Sir Thomas's portrait still presides over the parlor, which is said to be exactly as he left it. The furniture is of upright teak and there is a sofa which encourages no lounging. There are a few books: *London*, and *Certain Delightful English Towns*, together with *Hunting in India*. The titles supply their own commentary. Sir Thomas left behind some items of some worth in the mansion; these are now being catalogued by the monks who live there.

Sir Thomas left Sri Lanka when Independence was declared; Adisham was sold to a local lady. In 1960, she sold it to the Order of St Benedict. The house today is being put to full use and is maintained in beautiful condition. It is used as a chapter house for the monks, a retreat house for the religious and a hostel for visitors. The guest rooms are very good and the food is bound to be excellent, since the household tasks are one of the disciplines of the Benedictines. Certainly they make the best jam and marmalade you are likely to find in Sri Lanka. Visitors can buy a jar or two of their famous strawberry jam.

If you would like to stay in this haven of serenity, wit its English
garden full of flowers and well-cut lawns, its peaceful surroundings and
choice of walks, write to:

The Superior
St Benedict's Monastery
Adisham, Haputale.

Charges are extremely modest. Wait for confirmation of your
booking. No on-the-spot arrangements can be made.

Ella

A trip to the **Dunhinda Falls** is another must for visitors to the hills.
The road from Haputale goes up through ella, where it is worth making a
stop for lunch, or tea, or any excuse for that matter. Better still, stay there.
The Ella Rest House represents the best value accommodation
throughout the whole of Sri Lanka. It is situated amid beautiful
mountain scenery and the Rest House itself is well appointed. It is small,
with only 10 rooms, but these are charming and there is plenty of hot
water and clean towels, a rare combination in Sri Lanka. You can get a
room just by dropping in. It has a beautifully neat garden and a terrace
ideally situated for gazing down at the famous **Ella Gap** while sipping a
sunset drink. The food and service are excellent.

For the energetic there are many good walks, including one
which leads up the nearby ridge; magnificent views are afforded from
the top.

Badulla

Badulla is a delightful little town, boasting a number of
architecturally interesting houses with lushly growing gardens. The
town nestles in the hollow of a valley ringed by hills and dominated by
Namunukula Peak. Badulla is the main stopping point on the way to
Dunhinda Falls, the sixth highest in the world. When you go to
Dunhinda, take a picnic basket as the one kilometer or so hike goes
through some fine woodlands quite perfect for a picnic. It is a sweaty but
rewarding walk. The falls burst out with an explosion of white spray
which contrasts sharply with the surrounding green of the jungle. The
only thing that mars the natural beauty of the spot is the concrete
viewing-point erected by the Tourist Board.

All around the town of Badulla and particularly at the start of the
walk to Dunhinda, you will find stalls selling huge avocado pears and
chunks of newly chopped sandalwood. The avocados are delicious and
the sandalwood smells beautiful.

From Badulla you have a choice of routes. You can go to the east
coast through the **Lahugala Kitulana Sanctuary,** a leafy scenic route past
elephant meadows high with jungle grass. Or you can drive down to
Yala in the southeast corner and then on to the south coast at

Hambantota. Alternatively, you can wind you way back towards Colombo via Ratnapura.

If you take the south road to Hambantota, watch out for the **Rawana Falls** on the road past Ella. They are about five kilometers from Ella Gap on the Wellawaya Road. It was supposedly beneath these wild falls that Rawana imprisoned the unfortunate Sita, wife of Rama. You can see her little cave-home if you care to brave the water.

Beyond lie the **Diyaluma Falls**, reachable if you make a slight detour to the right before getting to Wellawaya. These are also among the highest waterfalls in Sri Lanka, about 168 m (560 ft) high. You can see them easily from the road and in fact it is best to stand on the opposite side to appreciate the arching fall of the waters.

The East Coast

Due to renewed fighting in the north and east in recent months, these areas are temporarily closed to visitors. For further information, please contact the Ceylon Tourist Board, PO Box 1504 Colombo, Sri Lanka or 228 Havelock Road Colombo, tel: 581801.

The main attractions of the East Coast are sea, sand and sun-bathing. There is not much else to do along this coast as it is not so richly endowed with sites of cultural interest. It draws mainly those who are looking for a place to laze away the days without worrying about the life they have temporarily left behind. Prices are generally reasonable.

Most people set out from **Trincomalee**, with its magnificent harbor, old temples and the nearby hot springs, although they tend to stay at **Nilaveli, Passekudah** or **Kalkudah** for sea, sun and sand. They might then go on to **Batticoloa**, noted for its sleepy lagoon and singing fish, where many people take an inland trip to the national park of **Gal Oya** to see the water birds, elephants, deer and a vast lake. The devoted sun-and-surf worshipers spend time at **Arugam Bay**, which is still undeveloped. Returning on the island road from Arugam Bay, the scenic road goes through the edge of the **Lahugala Kitulana Sanctuary** for elephants.

Trincomalee
This north-eastern coastal town is becoming more and more popular with visitors – not surprisingly, for it has a definite charm. Parts of the town are very gracious, especially the area around **Fort Frederick**. There are panoramic views from Trinco, as most people call it, down along the coast and out to sea. It boasts the second biggest natural harbor in the world and the bazaar area has a bustling cheerfulness.

The fact that when the west coast is suffering from monsoon rains, the east coast is not ensures there is always somewhere for the sun-seeker to go.

The countryside surrounding Trinco is very pastoral, with grazing cows and goats. The coconut palms grow taller here than on the southern coast, and vegetation is wild and bushy and not as domesticated as in the south. In Trinco itself, there is a beach, small, smooth and elegantly curved into a perfect half moon.

Trinco's most famous attribute is its harbor, one of the largest, safest and most beautiful in the world. During World War II, it served as the chief naval base for the entire South-East Asia and Far East Command and it remained a naval town for many years after that. It has a long and complex military history, stretching back to the early 17th century.

The fort still houses the militia, but it is also the main path up to the religious shrine of Swami Rock which is associated with Rawana, the demon in the Hindu epic, *Ramayana*. There are many references to Rawana in Sri Lanka, which has no national epic of its own but seems to share the *Ramayana*. Many folk stories claim that Rawana was an early Tamil king in Sri Lanka, and some even say he was the first Tamil king. He is said to have had the strength of 10 men and is often depicted with 10 heads. As you walk up to **Swami Rock**, you see on the right a big chunk of rock missing. This is called **Rawana's Gap**. An old tale says that Rawana was very much attached to his mother and resented her spending so much time at the spot in religious meditation. He therefore removed the rock, with his mother presumably still on it, and set it down beside him.

In the present temple, everything is new. Three hundred and fifty years ago, the Portuguese sent the main part of the old temple crashing down into the sea. Divers have found hundreds of statues, images and pillars in the depths. There is a seat on the rocks where people come to meditate and offer flowers and milk to the holy temple lying in the waters below.

The whole temple was reconstructed in 1958 and recently repainted. Brightly colored three-dimensional figures peer out of every pinnacle and corner. Some of the ancient images, which include a superb Vishnu and his consort, have been restored to the temple, thanks to the efforts of Arthur C. Clarke (the science-fiction writer who lives in Sri Lanka) and his team of divers.

There are several daily *pujas* (ceremonies of offering) to which outsiders and non-Hindus are welcome, provided they are hatless, shoeless and behave with respect. The times of the pujas are 6.45 am, 9 am, 11.45 am, 5 pm, 6 pm and 7.15 pm.

There are several possibilities for those wanting to visit other shrines.

About 13 km (eight miles) from Trincomalee, on a path extending beyond the Perkiyakulam tank (just short of Milepost 6 on the North Coast Road) is a Buddhist temple of unusual interest: **Velgam Vihara**, known to Hindus as **Natanar Kovil**. Dating from before the 2nd century, the buildings suffered damage during the Chola wars of the 11th century. But an inscription in site states that, during the Tamil Chola regime, Hindus helped restore it as a Buddhist shrine. Today it is Sri Lanka's one example of a Tamil vihara.

Much further along the North Coast Road – 48 km (30 miles) and two vehicular ferries – is the splendid 7th-century **vatagade** at **Tiriyai**, one of the three finest circular shrines on the island.

Southeast of Trincomalee, across the great Koddiyar Bay, is the celebrated site, **Seruwawila**. The dagaba there was built in the 3rd century BC by King Kavan Tissa to enshrine the frontal bone relic of the Buddha. On the way to Seruwawila, in the town of **Mutur**, is **Knox's Tree**. Somewhere here – the exact site is disputed – Robert Knox, King Rajasingha II's famous captive, author of the classic *Historical Relation of Ceylon* and co-inspirer with Alexander Selkirk of Defoe's *Robinson Crusoe*, was taken prisoner in 1660. Both places are inconvenient to reach by road – many wide ferries intervene – but a fairly regular launch service is maintained between Trincomalee and Mutur where there is a simple Rest House and where cars may be hired.

Trincomalee town offers a **Vishnu Temple,** one of the few such Hindu shrines in Sri Lanka, and **Wellington House** (in Fort Frederick) is .of interest. Over Christmas 1799, the Iron Duke, fresh from his victory over Tippu Sultan in South India, awaited transport to a new command in Egypt. Stricken ill, he missed his ship, which was lost with all hands in the Gulf of Aden. He had been saved for Waterloo! **Admiralty House** with its grassy gardens sweeping down to the Inner Harbour, its vast banyan tree and its quaint **Pepperpot Cottage** for the Flag Lieutenant, also housed famous men in its time: admirals ranging from Sir Charles Austen, Jane Austen's "problem" younger brother, to Dunhar-Nasmyth, the V.C. submariner of World War I.

Sir Charles is remembered by a monument in **St Stephen's Cemetery** overlooking the Outer Esplanade. There, also, is the tomb of P.B. Molesworth, the celebrated amateur astronomer and discoverer – while at Trincomalee – of the Red Spot on Jupiter. He lived (off Batticoloa Road) in a Siamese twin-style bungalow, a common dining room connecting identical wings. Here Molesworth and his brother, who could, it is said, neither bear to be parted nor abide each other for long, would meet only for meals, when a violent argument would temporarily separate them.

Trincomalee's greatest attraction for the average tourist will always be the sea and the jungle. The Inner Harbour, so deep and precipitous that it is thought to be volcanic in origin, affords safe swimming and boating in surroundings of splendor all year round. There are many picnic spots; the forlorn fairyland of **Round Island** (if you can land there) rising 500 fathoms from the sea-bottom in the very harbor mouth, whose charming Dutch name was Kyk in den Pot; **Great Sober Island** – the name is self-descriptive – with its tiny tranquil graveyard of sailors lost through seafaring accidents long ago; **Marble Bay** and **Dead Man's Cove**.

Excursions from Trincomalee

Kanniyai Hot Springs
The ride out to the **Kanniyai Hot Springs,** a pleasant eight-kilometer (five-mile) run out of Trinco, is enjoyable. These are the only hot springs in Sri Lanka in which it is possible to bathe. The others – at **Maha Oya** and at **Periyapullumalai** near Ampara – are boiling. There are seven small wells at Kanniyai with clear water, and six of them have slightly different temperature – 25°, 29°, 30°, 38°, 40°, and 45° Celsius (77°, 84°, 86°, 100°, 104° and 113° Fahrenheit). People reportedly come to these springs for their rheumatism and skin ailments, but a number of local people go there just to have hot baths, a rare luxury in a land of cold water.

Maha Oya
On the way back from the hot springs, you can visit a small **Veddah village** near the small town of Maha Oya. The Veddahs are believed to be the aboriginal people of Sri Lanka who live in the jungles. There are very few of them left now as most have intermarried with the Singhalese. They live in primitive huts and spend most of their time hunting the jungle's varied provender. The Veddahs hunt for nests of wild bees which hang high in the trees. They smoke out the bees and make off with the honey. Every Wednesday, they take their honey to the nearby town of Maha Oya and sell it. They are the only ones who sell genuine bee honey, rather than palm syrup. So if you are in Maha Oya on a Wednesday, drop in and buy some.

Nilaveli
Most people who stop in at Trinco actually stay at **Nilaveli,** where there are many hotels, rest houses, guest houses and small huts to stay in.

Nilaveli, in common with most coastal towns, has a lagoon. Local fishermen are usually delighted to take people on a lagoon trip, with a jungle trip extension. When arranging these trips, remember that the best time to go is either early morning or late afternoon. Moreover, if you are interested in seeing wildlife, you are wasting your money if you go at any other time. There are crocodiles in the Nilaveli lagoon.

Many boatmen try to lure visitors on a trip to **Pigeon Island** to see the coral. The best coral reefs are quite a long way beyond Pigeon Island and those who have been there say that it is a very impressive reef and teeming with fish, unlike the waters around Pigeon Island.

Local exports who know the East Coast well reluctantly reveal that by far the most unspoiled beaches lie further north, as does the lagoon of **Kokkilai;** this sanctuary for birds is also an ornithologist's heaven.

Batticoloa

Batticoloa means "muddy lagoon", but it is more picturesque than the Singhalese name would suggest. The town is famous for the singing fish. It is said that if you take a boat out to the middle of the lagoon on a moonlit night, you will hear mysterious singing. Many Batticoloa residents say they have never heard the alleged singing fish, but apparently there have been some recordings made of them. The singing is said to be like the ringing noise made by running a finger round the edge of a wet wine glass. Some people say that the noise is made by a certain kind of mollusk found on the rocks around the lagoon. Others maintain that the sound is at its loudest in the middle of the lagoon away from these rocks. Still others claim that the noise is a sort of wave echo from deep underground caves.

There is a little fort left behind by the fort-building Dutch which is now a local government office. The fort has become somewhat dingy, only distinguished by a couple of cannons. The town itself is slightly depressing, with an indifferent and grubby bazaar. There is also a Rest House but reports from other visitors regarding its rooms and food were not encouraging.

Passekudah and Kalkudah

These places are close to each other. **Passekudah** is more expensive than **Kalkudah**, but offers a good beach with various marine sports such as coral fishing, snorkeling, water-skiing, wind surfing and so on. For those interested in the more exotic side of oriental life, there is a Yoga Ashram at Kalkudah.

Arugam Bay

Arugam Bay is for sun-worshipers. There is nothing else to do but lie around in the sun, surf a while, and just live out a hedonistic existence. There are no shops (the nearest one are to be found in the little bus terminus of Pottuvil).

The roads around are full of wildlife. You may see a rare green-winged dove or a jungle fowl with its iridescent tail. People like to catch a young male fowl to mate with their own village hens so they can get rich red-yolked eggs instead of the almost-white yolked eggs served up ubiquitously in Sri Lanka. You may also come across the grey and rubbery Talogoya lizard which eats yams. You may also pass a star tortoise. It has a beautiful star-patterned carapace which has made it such a prize that the species has now had to be protected.

Arugam Bay boasts delightfully little huts on the shore but has too many undercurrents for anything other than careful bathing. Behind the palm-edged shore of the large curved bay lies a lagoon fringed by jungle. A lot of younger travelers stay at Arugam for its simplicity, its surf and, no doubt, for its cheapness. It is a charmingly unsophisticated place.

East Coast fishermen tend their nets on the beach at Nilaveli.

There are many good places to stay, but one which was highly recommended was Seasands.

Jaffna and The North

The area is temporarily closed to visitors. For further information please contact the Ceylon Tourist Board (page 110). In contrast to the lush green South, the countryside in the North is stark and dramatic, with a beauty of its own.

Tourists are sometimes discouraged from visiting the North, which is misconceived as being barren and unfriendly. This is because since Independence the Tamils have felt they have suffered considerably from being a minority. They have been pressing recently to become an independent state, and their demands for power have been backed by sporadic acts of violence from their more extreme members, the self-styled Tigers. This has caused hard feelings between predominantly Tamil North and the Singhalese South. The issue is complex and unlikely to be settled easily.

North of Anuradhapura, a dramatic change transforms the rural scene. Vegetation becomes more sparse and the landscape bolder. The road also passes through teakwood nurseries and Wilpattu, a national park noted for its leopards.

Jaffna is connected to the rest of Sri Lanka by a narrow isthmus known as **Elephant Pass**, so-called because elephants once used to wander there in search of young palmyrah palms. All round Elephant Pass are bleached salt pans; palmyrah palms, Jaffna's motif, still stand sentinel. The climate here is hotter and more humid than in the south. Once across Elephant Pass, the countryside changes again, and coconut palms and villages edge the road.

Jaffna is perched on a limestone shelf, and resultant geographical features are unique: limestone caverns at **Sinna** and **Periya Mandapam** extend inwards for about one kilometer (0.62 mile), while at **Neerveli** a well 43.5 m (142 ft) deep has been formed by the constant passage of tidal streams in and out of the rock. The well water of Neerveli is sweet near the surface but salty 30 m (99 ft) below. Fresh water springs also occur in many places.

Jaffna Town

Jaffna is a bright and attractive city, its chief charm being its atmosphere and way of life. Almost all the people are Tamils. These are the Jaffna Tamils, not to be confused with the so-called Indian Tamils who work on the tea estates. The Jaffna Tamils make their way in the world through hard work.

There is a very strong South Indian influence in Jaffna's culture and religion, evident in the many Hindu temples to be seen. A visit to the bazaar also gives a visit or the impression that he is in India. There are advertisement hoarding for Indian films, stalls selling bright saries and cheap imitation leather bags. You hear Indian film music from cassette players in the shops, and smell the sweetish scent of incense. The bazaar is colorful and offers many inexpensive items. No one tries to rip you off. Pause by any fruit stall and see if it has mangoes. Jaffna mangoes are said to be the best of the 500 varieties which grow in Sri Lanka.

Sights of Jaffna Town

Dutch Fort

The obvious place to begin your tour of Jaffna is with the excellently preserved **Dutch Fort**. Built in 1658, it is said to be the finest example of military fortification in Asia. Star-shaped, it is surrounded by wide ramparts which overlook a moat. It contains some buildings within the walls, but bears no resemblance to the village-style enclosures of Galle and Matara.

The fort was built upon the foundation of a Portuguese building, of which almost nothing remains. The block-like ramparts are made of white coral, which has now turned to greyish-black. On one corner of these you can see the remains of the gallows from which malefactors were hanged. The massive wooden doors are studded with metal spikes, apparently to withstand the attacks of elephants.

Just outside the fort is a little house where the author Leonard Woolf is said to have lived during part of his term of duty with the Ceylon Civil Service. His novel, *Village in the Jungle*, is sold at bookshops in Sri Lanka. It depicts life in a poor village, which in some ways has not changed greatly.

Dutch Church

The other notable features of the fort are the **Dutch Church**, or Groote Kerke, and the **Governor's Bungalow**. If you want to visit the church, call in first at the **Archaeological Museum** in town; an assistant will cycle with the massive key to open the church door and won't be averse to accepting a tip. Built in 1706, the church is in a poor state of preservation. The roof shows obvious signs of deterioration and the walls are dripping with damp. Nevertheless, it is still an imposing structure with a ponderous stylishness about it.

Governor's Bungalow

The big bungalow which served as the residence of the Dutch Governor of Jaffna still stands, with its rich dark antique furniture, such as four-poster beds and ancient armchairs with long arms intact. There are also few fine examples of china and porcelain which were once in general use. If you want to visit the bungalow, there is a watchman living nearby, and a member of his family can show you around.

Archaeological Museum

The Archaeological Museum, housed in an old Dutch building, has some interesting specimens of art objects, crafts and stonework which have been unearthed from various sites. There is a jawbone of a giant whale and some wood-carvings which are quite rare in Sir Lanka.

Many of the other vaunted attractions of Jaffna are scattered somewhat sparely around the peninsula. Everywhere you drive, the landscape is dominated by the striking palmyrah palm with its circle of leaves standing up around the head of the tree. This palm produces a large oval nut with a shiny brown casing. Unlike the coconut, it cannot be eaten or drunk, but it produces the very best toddy and has a number of uses besides. The palmyrah is said to be the palm with the widest geographical distribution, from Arabia to Timor, from India to Thailand. In Sri Lanka, it is found in other parts of the island but only in Jaffna are palmyrah plantations to be found.

Touring the peninsula

It need not take long to tour the peninsula. A morning drive will take you to the fresh water springs at Keerimalai. There is a rocky shore and a large tank in which you are likely to see old men soaping their withered flanks. By looking carefully, you can see the places where the fresh water springs bubble up into this channel.

From Keerimalai it is only a short drive along the coastal road to Point Pedro. On the beach stand fishermen painstakingly disentangling their nets and lines. Many of these fisherfolk live in temporary huts on the beaches, nomads ready to move to where the fishing is good. At Point Pedro a lighthouse marks the spot which used to be the main port for Jaffna.

You may be tempted by tourist literature to look for **Manalkadu**, which is claimed to be a mini-desert. In fact this consists only of palm trees on an area of sand beside the sea.

Offshore islands

Probably the greatest attractions for tourists are the islands off Jaffna. Each island has its own peculiar character and features. Some, such as **Kayts, Karaitivu** and **Punkudutivu**, are connected to the peninsula by motorable causeways.

On the way to Kayts, you will pass a Muslim mosque near the beach on the west coast. Here is the tomb of a Muslim holy man, called Abdul Abubakar, who used to heal the sick miraculously. Kayts was once the meeting place of Arab and Chinese traders who journeyed to Sri Lanka centuries ago for jewels and spices. Even Marco Polo was said to have visited Kayts. It is the sheltered harbor which accounts for this past popularity among foreign sailors. Kayts is a short ferry ride away from another Dutch fort called Hammenhiel.

The most famous of all the islands of Jaffna is **Delft**, named after the town in Holland. It is 12.8 km (eight miles) away from the city and is served by excellent ferries. The Dutch-style country house on the islands is an interesting relic of the Dutch occupation, originally built for the Captain of the Garrison in Delft. The Delft ponies are a curiosity. They are the result of a long period of horse-breeding initiated by the Portuguese more than 400 years ago.

It is virtually a full day's undertaking to visit Delft. Take your lunch with you as there is little to be bought on the island. Choose a sunny day so that you can sunbathe and swim once the few sights are seen.

Two uninhabited offshore islands, **Kachchativu** and **Palativu**, draw large numbers of pilgrims from India and Sri Lanka during the Roman Catholic festivals held in churches dedicated to St Anthony. The pilgrims come during a two-week period in February and March each year. Religion, whether Hindu, Muslim or Christian, plays an important role in the life of the people of Jaffna. One legend says that it was from Jaffna that one of the three Magi traveled to visit the infant Christ.

Temple and Churches

The Hindu kovils, dedicated to the deities of the vast Hindu pantheon, are the centers of some of the most ancient and colorful

Point Pedro.

festivals. Long processions, special performances of Carnatic music, fire-walking and various forms of penance are performed by pilgrims. These religious festivals attract not only pilgrims but also visitors. The **Kandasamy Kovil** in **Maviddapuram** draws pilgrims from Sri Lanka, India and other countries to its annual festival in July/August. The Kandasamy Kovil in **Nallur** hosts the longest and most colorful festival in the North, celebrating the arrival in Jaffna during the 15th century of a Singhalese king, Bhuvaneka Bahu VI of Kotte. The huge car (called a Juggernaut) used in the procession is one of the finest extant examples of Hindu wood-carving. The festival at **Nagapooshani Ammal Kovil** on the island of Nainativu is likewise spectacular. And the Nagatambiran Kovil at Nagarkovil re-enacts the legendary battle between the Portuguese and the Serpent God.

The small festivals too are occasions of color and music. You may come upon a procession in which the gods are led out of the temple and through the streets. No one minds visitors taking an interest and sometimes the participants are happy to pose for pictures.

Most of the ancient Hindu temples and monuments of Jaffna are gone, removed with Portuguese missionary zeal in the 16th and 17th centuries. What remains are a few ruins of sacred shrines in ancient sites.

There are also a number of sites which are of great significance to Buddhists, although they form the minority in Jaffna. Of these, the Naga Dipa Vihara on the island of Nainativu is the most famous. It was built before the advent of Buddhism in Sri Lanka, and is believed to have been consecrated during one of the Buddha's three visits to the island.

For those interested in Christian structures, there are some good examples of Portuguese ecclesiastic architecture in the ruins of a large building with a stone-roofed apse at **Chankanai** and in a fine Romanesque ruin in Myliddy.

Beaches

There are excellent beaches and lovely, unspoiled areas for those interested in marine life. Worth visiting is **Kalmunai Point**, a beautiful and wild headland reached by boat. The safest time to visit is during the north-east monsoon, roughly from February to June.

Casuarina Beach in **Karainagar** is somewhat over-rated. It does not offer, as it is claimed, kilometres of excellent beaches. It has one particularly good strip of 450 m (1,476 ft) long in front of the hotels. It is kept clean and tidy for the tourists and is opposite the coral reef which can be seen either by taking a glass-bottomed boat or by snorkeling there. This reef is particularly good for spotting multicolored tropical fish. It is best to do this between 9 am and 1 pm.

You can go skin-diving at **Eluvaitivu Shoal**, off Eluvaitivu Island. There are underwater caves at depth of 4.5 m (14.7 ft) downwards which you can explore, but take an underwater torch with you. Around this area, you may well get the chance to dive with the professional Tamil fishermen of the *chank* caste who g down for bright tropical fish which they then sell for export. It is not suitable for snorkeling here as the water is too deep.

There is talk that the hotels in this area will be offering water-skiing and sailing facilities, but at the time of writing these are not available.

The North is rich in wildlife. For those with botanic interests, there are the big fat baobabs of Delft and everywhere around Jaffna the green shelter of the Honduras mahogany trees.

For bird-watchers, there are migrant Caspian terns, black-headed gulls, oyster catchers, and field storks. In Jaffna itself you will see the white-bellied sea eagle and at the rather more inaccessible **Chundikulam Bird Sanctuary** they have flamingos and a wealth of other feathered residents.

Other things to keep your eyes open for in Jaffna are the wells worked by buffalo walking round in a circle and the cadjan fences and thatched roofs made of palmyrah leaves.

Where to Stay

Jaffna does not have much to offer in the way of accommodation. The choice is between the rather expensive **Ashok Hotel** and the rather grubby **Subhas Hotel.** However, the food at the Ashok is cheaper and better than that at the Subhas. Other accommodation can be found in local homes by asking around.

The Wildlife Parks

There is no doubt that Sri Lanka has an extraordinary variety of wildlife and it is by no means confined to the national parks or wildlife conservation areas.

For bird watchers, the countryside is a paradise. There are over 425 species, of which a number are migrants arriving in October and staying until March. The best places for observing birds are not the actual wildlife parks which tend to suffer form over-visitation, but in the villages, fields and quiet rural corners of Sri Lanka.

Most parts of the coast are richly endowed with marine life, from brightly colored tropical fish to sea turtles, coral gardens and shellfish. The lagoons just inland are the natural home of water birds, giant water monitor lizards and even crocodiles.

All that is quite apart from the wildlife parks which shelter elephants, leopards, deer, monkeys and all kinds of bird, reptile and insect life.

Any drive along any road will reveal an astonishing variety of creatures – mongooses scuttering into the undergrowth, lizards sunning on tree stumps, snakes sidling away, peacocks strutting about, and the beautiful and endangered star tortoise ambling slowly across the road. However, although this wildlife may look lavish, it is in as much danger of extinction in Sri Lanka as anywhere else in the world. Every day, through greed or carelessness or environmental change, their numbers decrease.

The tropical rainforest has practically disappeared. Only a portion remains in the **Sinharaja Rain Forest** and even that is threatened by mechanized logging. Less than nine percent of the area of the Wet Zone is now forested and this is decreasing. Slopes, hills and water-courses are being cleared, and soil erosion is resulting.

The sea is being over-fished, and coral reefs which take millions of years to form are being broken up daily for the production of lime. Tropical fish are exported by the millions and sea turtles and dugongs – those legendary mermaids beloved of sailors – are in danger of extinction.

Poaching is still an all too common occurrence, despite the stringent government action that is taken against poachers. Often it is the tourist market that is the destination for these illegitimate trappings.

Take care not to buy anything which contravenes the laws on protected species. If you do, you will have trouble with the Customs when you try to leave the country. More important, you will be contributing to the further destruction of one of Sri Lanka's most valuable attributes – its wildlife.

The following are protected: leopard, gerbil or antelope rat, pangolin, loris, green turtle, elephant, palm civet, fishing cat, buffalo, flying squirrel, star tortoise, hog or swamp deer, mouse deer, crocodile,

jungle cat, water monitor, sloth bear, bear monkey or highland purple-faced leaf monkey, hawkbill turtle, barking deer or red deer, spotted deer, python, dugong and sambhur.

You cannot export any part of any of the above creatures – not the skin, bone, horn, teeth, paws or shell. Neither should you accept gifts of any of the above, live or dead, whole or part. Even if it means an awkward moment, refuse politely and explain why you must refuse. Many villagers are ignorant of the protection laws and it is no bad thing to help ensure that they get to know about them.

If live animals interest you then a trip to a national park is a rewarding experience. There are several major national parks, and many smaller conservation areas. Sri Lanka has a long and honorable history with regard to conservation; it had one of the first game reserves in the history of mankind. Today ten percent of the government's land is devoted to the conservation of wildlife.

However, if your interest in wildlife is only casual, it is better that you avoid the national parks. All of them are suffering greatly from over-visitation, and some parks have been temporarily closed to give the animals and birds a rest from the constant prying of tourists. If you just want to look at animals and birds, go to Dehiwela Zoo outside Colombo.

If you have a keener interest in the natural environment, and want a special trip arranged, the Wildlife and Nature Protection Society of Sri Lanka will help you. The name is self-explanatory and the Society will be pleased to arrange an itinerary for one or more, with an expert guide and all other details taken care of. Unlike the commercial firms which profess to offer the same services, the Society is non-profit-making and any expenses involved will be the minimum possible. Your guide will be a member of the Society and therefore a real expert in the field you want – whether that be marine life, jungle life, birds, insects, reptiles or whatever else interests you. The only condition is that you agree to join the Society, which costs a mere Rs.25 annually.

Write to: The Secretary, Wildlife and Nature Protection Society of Sri Lanka, Chaitiya Road, Colombo 1 (Telephone: 25248).

The two most famous of the wildlife parks are the **Yala National Park** and the **Wilpattu National Park**. Gal Oya is a park of special interest to bird-watchers. A complete list of all the wildlife conservation areas is available from the Wildlife Conservation Department, near the Dehiwela Zoo, outside Colombo.

Yala

Yala is called that by everyone, even though its official name is Ruhunu. The name change came in 1938 and never caught on.

This is the country's premier wildlife refuge, all 1,259 sq km (486 sq miles) of it. It is best known for its 2,500 elephants but Yala

(preceding page) An avenue of trees in the Peradeniya Botanical Gardens.

also has a goodly sized population of bears, leopards, deer, sambhur and wild boars. Numerous water birds live around the lagoons and lakes, while the forest shelters hornbills, flycatchers, barbets, orioles and other birds and the plains are overrun by peafowl and quail.

The park is 309 km (192 miles) from Colombo and can be reached by the coastal route through Bentota and Devinuwara at the southern extreme of the island or via the highland route through Ratnapura. On both roads, the last major town is **Tissamaharama** – another bird-watcher's dream – and from there the turn-off on the **Kirinda road** is only eight kilometers (five miles) away. The Park Office is in the tiny hamlet of **Palatupana**, 12.8 km (eight miles) further on. The casual visitor should try to get in for the full day, or at least from 4 pm until 6 pm when most animals come to the water-holes to drink.

Different animals in Yala have different haunts. Elephants gather at **Uraniya**, leopards at **Wepandeniya Rock**, bears at **Jamburagala**, sambhur along the sand dunes, and spotted deer on the **Buttuwa Plains**. There is a reasonable chance of seeing some representatives of most of these species. After all, there are the 2,500 elephants (six percent of them male tuskers), about 1,000 bears, 600 leopards and countless numbers of other species.

Better than a day trip, consider staying overnight in Yala. There are six furnished bungalows, each capable of accommodating up to eight people. A cook is provided. Linen can be hired and guides are free. For larger groups, tents big enough for 10 persons each. Visitors to these last two must take their own bedding and cook their own meals, but it would be easy to hire someone in the district for a modest sum. Prices for accommodation are very cheap, but it is necessary to write well ahead for reservations.

Write to: Department of Wildlife Conservation, Transwork House, Lower Chatham Street, Colombo 1, tel: 34040.

Wilpattu

Wilpattu covers an area of 1,908 sq km (737 sq miles) and lies along the north-west coast between the **Modaragam River** and the **Kala Oya**. It is particularly famous for its leopard population.

The name Wilpattu derives from *villu*, meaning a shallow in the ground which becomes a pond or lake. There is a collection of such villus in the middle of the park and they are famed for the birdlife around them. It is necessary to drive there in a jeep and the jungle scenery on the way is very impressive.

As well as its abundant wildlife, Wilpattu also boasts some remarkable ruins, among a 5th-century dagaba. Rumors also tell of a huge standing Buddha once found in the depths of the jungle by two men who could not trace their way back to it again.

There is also excellent cheap accommodation within Wilpattu, which again must be hired through the Wildlife Conservation Department in Colombo.

The approach to the park is on the Puttalam-Anuradhapura Road, and the turn-off is well signposted.

Gal Oya

At the center of Gal Oya is a huge artificial lake formed in 1956 as part of a giant hydro-electric scheme to develop the area. The skeletons of thousands of dead trees, drowned in the making of Gal Oya, edge the shallows of the lake, making it look like the surface of a dead planet. The lake has become home to thousands of water birds. It is quite a sight to behold 100,000 black cormorants sweeping up into the sky with a great clapping of wings. In addition to cormorants, fat pelicans, sea eagles and other water birds, there are also a few shy elephants occasionally to be seen lurking on land, and herds of hairy wild buffalo dozing in the water.

The only way to visit Gal Oya, at the time of writing, was by hiring a boat from a privately-owned travel firm whose monopoly of the market probably accounts for the high prices. Most of these boats are hired through the Safari Inn, owned by the same company. The Inn is likewise in a position to exploit, being the only accommodation in the immediate area of Gal Oya, and standards are consequently very poor.

Check with other guests and tourists if they would like to share a boat trip with you. The Inn will tell you that no one wants to share with you, as this increases the number of trips they can make in a day; in fact there is usually a good chance of cooperation with other guests.

A warning: The Inn also runs another trip by jeep to a **Vedda village**. It is advertised as a jungle trip and you will be told the track there is impassable otherwise. Not true. The village is called Veddagama (Vedda Village) and is about 37 km (23 miles) away, navigable by an ordinary car.

Directions: Leave the Safari Inn and drive to the roundabout, where you turn right. Continue for a few kilometers, across an orange bridge which edges the side of the road, then turn left at a second bridge. Cross it and drive straight ahead until you come to a small post office building. There, by the general store, you will find some local people who will be more than happy to direct you the rest of the way for a small tip. You will have to take some betel to present to the Vedda headman and you will have to pay for any photographs you take. If it is possible, buy some wild honey. It is the best in Sri Lanka.

Do not be surprised if your hire-car driver assures you that the road to the Veddah village can only be reached by jeep. That is because he gets

A peacock in the Wilpattu National Park.

a fat commission out of what you pay the hotel for the trip. Just assure him that the road is navigable.

If you know you will want to visit the national parks of Sri Lanka, try to find out before hand if they are open or not. Many visitors are very disappointed to find them closed. The periods of closure can begin at any time, continue for several weeks, and be extended beyond the originally stated date.

Recommended Reading

There are many ways to learn about any country and one very good one is to read books about it. The first, longest and oldest series of writing about Sri Lanka are the *Chronicles, Greater and Lesser*. These two extraordinary works were written over the course of 2,000 years by the monks and scholars of the Singhalese Buddhist community. The Greater Chronicle (the *Mahavamsa*) starts with the founding of the Sinhala race in 550 BC, and the Lesser Chronicle (the *Chulavamsa*) finished in 1815 when the British took the island. Written in Pali, they have been translated into vivid and evocative English by the Pali Text Society and the Sri Lankan government. Out of print, they are available in Sri Lanka at shocking prices, but are well worth buying for all that. It is not many countries that have a written history that long.

More modern but equally good in its own way is Major Roland Raven-Hart's *Ceylon: A History in Stone*. Raven-Hart lived for many years in the country and really knew his stuff. His book is a marvelous way to supplement any guidebook. It is scholarly, entertaining and the result of many years' work. Published by Lake House, it is available in bookshops. It is about to be reprinted at a new price.

A classic is Sir James Emerson Tennant's *Ceylon*, a bumper two-volume affair in facsimile, published by Tisara Prakasakayo, a house which does some excellent reproductions of old books. Tennant wrote in the 1850s, but much of his information is still valid and has not been bettered. It is thoroughly recommended.

A modern writer of real value is Maureen Seneviratne, whose book, *Some Mahavamsa Places*, really brings ancient times alive again. This too is highly recommended. Two new publications worth buying are *A Guide to Anuradhapura* and *A Guide to Polonnaruwa*, written by Nigel and Caroline Palmer. They are recommended for anyone wanting a really reliable and interesting account of the ancient cities. Buy these and you won't need any other guide to them. You will also be helping to raise money for the Cultural Triangle Project (see p.71).

Appendix

Accommodation

This is a list of the accommodation registered with and approved by the Ceylon Tourist Board. That does not mean that it is all of the best quality. Tourism in Sri Lanka has been subject to great inflation. There are too many people in search of a fast buck, a number of whom are hoteliers.

The best value accommodation in Sri Lanka is provided by private families. These have nice clean rooms and cater for a very small number of guests. such places do have European-style toilets, clean and simple rooms. You will certainly get good food. Some people complain that some of the places listed as guest houses are rather like seedy English boarding houses and offer an awful lot of overcooked cabbage in their meals. Be adventurous and find your own places to stay too.

Most accommodation units other than the inexpensive accommodation units, have three rates: Room only, bed and breakfast and all inclusive. Inquire from hotel, guest house or rest house for relevant tariff. A 10% service charge is added to the bill in most places.

Abbreviations: R/O – Room Only; B/B – Bed and Breakfast; A/I – All Inclusive; A/C – Air-Conditioned; Non A/C – Non Air-Conditioned; SWB – Single with Bath. The number before these symbols indicates number of rooms.

We have classified the hotels' prices as Budget (B), Moderate (M), Expensive (E), and Very Expensive (VE). Please note that with inflation in the tourist industry in Sri Lanka, price range is merely an indicator of the level of accommodation. Prices change upwards continually. If you feel that standards and service are below what you would expect, write and say so to the Ceylon Tourist Board.

AMBALANGODA: *Guests Houses*

Randomba Inn   R/O (B)
738-740 Galle Road
Randomba
Tel: 097-406

Blue Horizon Tour Inn   B/B (B)
129 Main Street
Ambalangoda
Tel: 097-475

ANURADHAPURA: *Hotels*

Ashok Hotels   R/O (B)
Rowing Club Road
Anuradhapura
Tel: 587652

Miridiya   50 R/O (M)
Rowing Club Road
Anuradhapura
Tel: 025-2112 or 2519

Nuwarawewa Rest House   60 R/O A/I (M)
New Town, Anuradhapura
Tel: 565 Anuradhapura
Contact tel: 025-2565

Rajarata   100 R/O A/C B/B (VE)
Rowin Club Road
Anuradhapura
Tel: 025-2578

Tissawewa Rest House   25 R/O A/I (M)
Old Town, Anuradhapura
Tel: 025-2299
Contact tel: 583133 Colombo
(Beautiful setting, good service and food)

Guests Houses
Hela Inn   4 R/O (B)
Ratnayakepura
Anuradhapura
(Excellent food)

Hotel Monara   9 R/O (B)
Freeman Mawatha
Anuradhapura
Tel: 210 Anuradhapura

Shanthi   R/O (B)
891 Mailagas Junction
Anuradhapura
Tel: 515 Anuradhapura

BADULLA :
Dunhinda Falls Inn   20 R/O (B)
35/11 Bandaranayake Mawatha
Badulla
Tel: 406 Badulla

BALANGODA :
Gem Rest Guest Inn   R/O A/I (B)
Ratmalawinne
Balangoda

BANDARAWELA : *Hotels*
Bandarawela Hotel   36 R/O A/I (M)
Bandarawela
Tel: 501 Bandarawela

Guests Houses
Alpine Inn   R/O (B)
Ellatota
Bandarawela
Tel: 569 Bandarawela

Ideal Resort   R/O (B)
Welimada Road
Bandarawela
Tel 476 Bandarawela

BENTOTA : *Hotels*
Bentota Beach   135 A/C R/O (VE)
Bentota
Tel: 034-75266

Hotel Ceysands   84 R/O A/I (E)
Bentota
Tel: 034-75073
Contact tel: 20862 Colombo

Lihiniya Surf Hotel   86 A/C A/I B/B (E)
National Holiday Resort
Bentota
Tel: 034-75126/9 and 75486

Serendib National Holiday Resort
Bentota   77 B/O (M)
Tel: 034-75248, 75313
Contact tel: 32895 Colombo

Guest House
Dilmini Tourist   5 R/O (B)
Guest House
Welipanne Road
Aluthgama
Tel: 048-5230

BERUWELA : *Hotels*
Barberyn Reef   40 B/B A/I (E)
Beruwela
Tel: 034-75220

Bayroo Beach Hotel   42 A/I B/B (VE)
Beruwela
Tel: 034-75297

Confifi Beach Hotel   60 Non A/C (VE)
Beruwella   A/C B/B
Tel: 034-75217

Hotel Swanee   52 B/B A/I (E)
Moragalla
Beruwela
Tel: 034-75213
Contact tel: 21101

Neptune   92 B/B A/I (VE)
Moragalla
Beruwela
Tel: 034-75218, 75219, 75301

Palm Garden   120 B/B A/I (VE)
Moragalla
Beruwela
Tel: 034-75263

Pearl Beach   40 B/B F/B (M)
Beruwela
Tel: 034-75117, 75118

Guest Houses
Berlin Bear   10 B/B (M)
Maradana, Beruwela
Tel: 048-5525

BIBILE : *Guest Houses*
Bibimo Motel   5 (B)
54 Badulla Road
Bibile

COLOMBO : *Hotels*
Ceylinco   15 R/O (VE)
69 Janadhipathi Mawatha
Colombo1
Tel: 20431-3

Galle Face 141   SWB R/O (VE)
2 Kollupitiya Road
Colombo 3
Tel: 541010 (7 lines)

Havelock Tourinn 32 A/C R/O (VE)
20 Dickmans Road
Colombo 5
Tel: 85251-3

Holiday Inn 100 A/C R/O (VE)
30 Sir Mohamed Macan Marker
Mawatha, Colombo 3
Tel: 22001-9

Hotel Brighton 62 A/C R/O (E)
57 Ramakrishna Road
Colombo 6
Tel: 585211-2

Hotel Ceylon 250 A/C R/O (VE)
Inter-Continental
48 Janadhipathi Mawatha
Colombo 1
Tel: 21221

Hotel Ceylon Inns 74 A/C R/O (E)
501 Galle Road B/B
Colombo 6
Tel: 83336-8

Hotel Duro 27 B/B R/O (M)
429 Kollupitiya Road
Colombo 3
Tel: 585338, 585335, 581772

Hotel Empress 35 B/B (M)
383 R.A. De Mel Mawatha
Colombo 3
Tel: 574930-1

Hotel Janaki 70 Non A/C (M)
43 Fife Road A/C R/O
Colombo 5
Tel: 81524, 85336

Hotel Lanka Oberoi 376 A/C R/O (VE)
77 Steuart Place
Colombo 3
Tel: 20001, 21171

Hotel Sapphire 40 A/C R/O (M)
371 Galle Road A/C Suite
Colombo 6
Tel: 583306

Hotel Taprobane 61 R/O (M)
York Street, Colombo 1
Tel: 20391-4

Hotel Ranmuthu 54 R/O (M)
112 Galle Road
Colombo 3
Tel: 33986, 33988-9

The Pegasus Reef 144 R/O (E)
Santha Maria Mawatha
Hendala, Wattala
Tel: 530250/8

Renuka Hotel 43 R/O (VE)
328 Kollipitiya Road
Colombo 3
Tel: 573598

Rio Grand Hotel A/C R/O (M)
60 Kumaran Ratnam Road
Colombo 2
Tel: 24863, 32926

Sea View Hotel 22 R/O (B)
15 Sea View Avenue
Colombo 3
Tel: 26516

Silver Bird Hotel 22 R/O (B)
8, 42nd Lane, Galle Road
Colombo 8
Tel: 83143

Guest Houses
Chanuka 13 R/O B/B (B)
29 Francis Road
Colombo 6
Tel: 85883

Colombo Guest House 7 B/B (M)
26 Charles Place A/C B/B
Colombo 3
Tel: 33402

Cubile Mare A/C R/O (B)
Uswetekeiyawa
Tel: 25984, 36433

Halwa Tourist Inn 3 A/C B/B (B)
50/3 Sir Marcus Fernando Mawatha
Colombo 7
Tel: 92265

Hill Top Holiday Inn 11 A/C B/B (B)
51 High Level Road
Homagama
Tel: 36862 or 0793-297

Lanka Inns   20 B/B A/I (B)
239 Galle Road
Colombo 4
Tel: 84220

Lake Lodge   16 B/B (B)
20 Alwis Terrace
Colombo 3
Tel: 26443

Orchid Inn   29 R/O B/B (B)
571/6 Galle Road
Colombo 6
Tel: 583916

Omega Inn   15 A/C R/O (B)
324 Galle Road   Non A/C R/O
Colombo 6
Tel: 582277, 585604, 587820

Ottery Inn   8 B/B (B)
29 Melbourne Avenue
Colombo 4
Tel: 83727

St. Georges   6 R/O (B)
43 Peterson Lane
Colombo 6
Tel: 88545

Sonnenschien   12 A/C R/O (B)
187 Ward Place   Non A/C R/O
Colombo 7
Tel: 94594

Star Inns   10 R/O (B)
73/22 Sri Saranankara Road
Dehiwela
Tel: 71-4030/6999

Sivali Palace   4 /B (B)
581 Sivali Palace
Pita Kotte
Tel: 074-2788

World Trade & Tourist Centre
237 Galle Road   12 A/C R/O (B) A/C Suites
Colombo 4
Tel: 580542, 580543

Y.M.C.A. International Guesthouse   (B)
393 Union Place
Colombo 2
Tel: 24694, 22196

DICKOYA : *Guest Houses*
Upper Glencairn   5 R/O B/B (B)
Dickoya
Tel: 0512-348

GALLE : *Hotels*
New Oriental   30 R/O B/B (M)
10 Church Street
Fort, Galle
Tel: 09-22059

Guest Houses
Closenberg   8 R/O (M)
Magalle, Galle
Tel: 09-3073

Harbour Inn   4 A/I (M)
Bonavista
Unawatuna, Galle
Tel: 09-2822, 23504

Orchard Holiday Home   5 R/O (B)
61 Light House Street
Fort, Galle
Tel: 09-2370, 84473

Unawatuna Beach Resort   4 R/O B/B (B)
Parangiyawatta, Unawatuna
Tel: 09-22147

GAL OYA : *Guest Houses*
Inginiyagala Safari Inn   R/O B/B (B)
Inginiyagala
Tel: 826 Inginiyagala

GIRITALE : *Hotels*
Giritale Hotel   44 R/O B/B (M)
National Holiday Resort
Giritale
Tel: 027-6311, contact tel: 25984

Hotel Hemalee   10 R/O B/B (B)
Polonnaruwa Road, Giritale
Tel: 027-6257

Royal Lotus Hotel   54 A/C R/O B/B (M)
Giritale
Tel: 027-6316

HABARANA : *Hotels*
Habarana Walk Inn 106 Non A/C R/O A/I (E)
Habarana
Tel: 27206-8 or
Habarana 11 & Dambulla 316

HIKKADUWA : *Hotels*
Blue Corals   60 A/C R/O (M)
332 Galle Road
Tel: 09-22679

Coral Gardens   50 R/O
Hikkaduwa
Tel: 09-23023, 22189

Coral Reef Beach   30 R/O B/B (B)
Hikkaduwa
Tel: 37 Hikkaduwa

Coral Sands   60 B/B F/B (M)
326 Galle Road
Hikkaduwa
Tel: 09-22436
Contact tel: 583851

Hotel Lanka   24 B/B (M)
Super Coral
Hikkaduwa
Tel: 09-22897

Guest Houses
Coral Seas Beach Resort   9 B/B (M)
346 Colombo Road
Hikkaduwa
Tel: 09-3248

Poseidon Diving Station   R/O (M)
Galle Road
Hikkaduwa
Tel: 894 Hikkaduwa

Seaside Inn   10 R/O B/B (B)
Patuwata, Dodanduwa
Contact tel: 097-337

HORTON PLAINS : *Guest Houses*
Anderson Lodge   R/O (B)
Horton Plains
Contact tel: 33012, 33787

Farr's Inn   9 A/I (M)
Horton Plains
Contact tel: 23501/23504

HORANA : *Guest House*
Wasana Tourist Inn   5 R/O (B)
Hegalla Estate
Horana
Tel: 209

Jaffna *Hotels*
Subhas   50 R/O (M)
15 Victoria Road
Jaffna
Tel: 7228 Jaffna

Palm Court   10 R/O B/B (B)
202 Main Street
Jaffna
Tel: 628 Jaffna

KALUTARA : *Hotels*
Merivier   72 B/B R/O (E)
Katukurunda
Kalutara
Tel: 034-22530

KANDY : *Hotels*
chalet   27 B/B A/I (M)
32 Gregory's Road
Kandy
Tel: 08-4353

Lady Hill   40 R/O B/B (M)
Dangolla
Kandy
Tel: 08-2659
Contact tel: 32895 Colombo

Hotel Casamara   35 A/C B/B A/I (M)
12 Kotugodella Veediya
Kandy
Tel: 08-24051, 24052, 24053

Hotel Dehigama   20 R/O B/B (M)
84 Raja Veediya
Kandy
Tel: 08-2709

Hotel Hantana   35 R/O B/B (M)
Hantana Road
Kandy
Tel: 08-23067

Hotel Suisse   64 R/O A/I (M)
30 Sangaraja Mawatha
Kandy
Tel: 08-22637

Hotel Topaz   50 R/O B/B (M)
Anniwatte
Kandy
Tel: 08-24150, 23061 or
Colombo 81191

Hunas Falls   22 R/O A/I (E)
Elkaduwa, Kandy
Tel: 20716, 29964 Colombo

Mahaweli Beach   23 R/O B/B (M)
33 Siyambalagastenne Road
Kandy
Tel: 08-32062

Queens   90 R/O F/B (M)
Dalada Veediya, Kandy
Tel: 08-22121/2

Guest Houses
Castle Hill   4 B/B (M)
22 Gregory's Road
Kandy
Tel: 08-4376

The Dawn Tourist Inn   B/B (M)
124 Mapanawathura Road
Kandy
Tel: 08-3923

The Fair Heavens   B/B (M)
47 Sir Cuda Ratwatte Mawatha
Kandy
Tel: 08-3555

Grass Mere Farm   2 B/B (M)
Alupothuwela, Uruwela
Tel: 0662-394

Greenwoods   R/O (B)
Alikandawatte, Elahera

Riverdale   15 R/O B/B (M)
32 Anniwatte Road
Kandy
Tel: 08-3020

Rubaiyat   22 B/B (E)
532/6, Sieble Place
Kandy
Tel: 08-3080

Sandy River Inn   9 B/B (B)
14/1, Deveni Rajasinghe Mawatha
Getambe — Tel: 08-2585

Hotel Thilanka   33 R/O (M)
3 Sangamitta Mawatha
Kandy
Tel: 08-22060

Windy Cot   30 R/O B/B (B)
66 Riverdale Road
Aniwatte, Kandy
Tel: 08-22052

Zeylanica   B/B A/I (B)
2 Mahamaya Mawatha
Kandy
Tel: 08-24388

KEGALLE : *Guest House*
Concept Randeniya   5 R/O (B)
Tel: 296 Rambukkana

KOGGALA : *Hotels*
Hotel Horizon   70 Non A/C A/I (M)
Koggalla, Habaraduwa   A/C A/I
Tel: 09-53297 Habaraduwa

Koggala Beach   204 B/B A/I (M)
Koggala, Habaraduwa
Tel: 09-53260, 53243

Hotel Beach Haven   B/B (M)
Talpe
Tel: 09-2663, 076-321

MATALE : *Guest House*
Matale Tourist Guest House 10 B/B R/O (B)
145 Moysey Crescent Road
Matale
Tel: 259 Matale

MATARA : *Hotels*
Polhena Reef Gardens Hotel 20 R/O B/B (B)
30 Beach Road Polhena
Tel: 041-2478

Guest House
Maheeka Tourist Inn   R/O A/I (B)
363 Meddawatha
Matara
Tel: 041-2131

MOUNT LAVINIA : *Hotels*
Mt. Lavinia Hotel   180 A/C R/O (E)
Hotel Road
Mt Lavinia
Tel: 071-5221, 5521-22-23

Palm Beach   46 B/B A/I (E)
52 De Saram Road
Mt. Lavinia
Tel: 71-2711

Saltaire Beach Resort 12 R/O (M)
50/2 De Saram Road
Mt Lavinia
Tel: 71-7786

Tillys Beach Hotel 69 R/O (M)
200 Soysa Avenue, Mt. Lavinia
Tel: 71-3531/33

Rivi Ras 50 R/O A/C (E)
50/2 De Saram Road
Mt Lavinia
Tel: 71-7786, 7731

Guests Houses
Concord 21 B/B (B)
131-141 Galle Road
Dehiwela
Tel: 71-7727

Estoril Tourist Lodge 22 B/B (M)
5/2 Lilian Avenue
Mt. Lavinia
Tel: 71-5494

Marina Nivasa 16 B/B (B)
30 Sri Dharmapala Road
Mt Lavinia
Tel: 71-7337

Mt. Lavinia Holiday Inn 7 B/B (B)
17 De Saram Road
Mt. Lavinia
Tel: 71-7187

Hanveli Beach Resort 24 B/B (M)
56/9 De Saram Road
Mt. Lavinia
Tel: 71-7385

San Michel 11 B/B (B)
Deltara, Piliyandala
Tel: 22566

Sea Breeze Tour Inn 23 B/B M)
De Saram Road R/O
Mt. Lavinia
Tel: 71-4017

NEGOMBO : *Hotels*
Blue Lagoon 60 R/O (VE)
Talahena A/C R/O
Negombo
Tel: 031-2380

Blue Oceanic Beach Hotel 50 A/C R/O (E)
Ethukala, Negombo
Tel: 031-2377, 2642

Browns Beach Hotel 90 A/C R/O (M)
175 Lewis Place
Negombo
Tel: 031-2031/2

Catamaran Beach 22 R/O (M)
89 Lewis Place
Negombo
Tel: 031-2342

Dons Beach 62 R/O B/B (E)
75 Lewis Place
Negombo
Tel: 031-2120, 2448

Golden Beach 50 R/O B/B (M)
161 Lewis Place
Negombo
Tel: 031-2113, 2631

Goldi Sands 64 R/O (B)
Ethukala
Negombo
Tel: 031-2021, 2348, 2627

Ranweli Holiday Village 84 B/B F/B (VE)
Waikkal
Kochchikade
Tel: 031-2136

Sea Shell 64 R/O A/I (B)
Palangaturai
Kochchikade
Tel: 031-2062, 3368

Sun Flower 45 B/B A/I (E)
143 Lewis Place
Negombo
Tel: 031-2042

Guest Houses
Golden Haven 9 B/B F/B (B)
Kimbulpitiya
Negombo
Tel: 031-2324

Hotel Sea Gardens 15 B/B R/O (B)
Ethukalah
Negombo
Tel: 031-2150

Hotel Wind Mill Beach Resort B/B H/B (B)
Ethukalah
Negombo
Tel: 031-2572

Interline Beach Hotel 7 R/O B/B (B)
65/3 Seneviratne Mawatha
Lewis Place
Negombo
Tel: 031-2350

Rainbow 8 B/B (B)
2 Carron Place
Negombo
Tel: 031-2082

Sea Drift 4 R/O B/B (B)
2 Carron Place
Negombo
Tel: 031-2350

The Silver Sands 18 B/B (B)
95 Lewis Place
Negombo
Tel: 031-2402

NUWARA ELIYA : *Hotels*
St. Andrews Hotel 32 R/O B/B (M)
Nuwara Eliya
Tel: 0522-445

Grand Hotel 102 R/O B/B (M)
Nuwara Eliya
Tel: 0522-881

Grosvenor 19 B/B H/B (B)
Nuwara Eliya
Tel: 0522-307

Hill Club (B)
Nuwara Eliya
Tel: 0522-305

Princess Guest House B/B R/O (B)
12 Wedderburn Road
Nuwara Eliya
Tel: 462 Nuwara Eliya
Contact tel: 31398

PASSEKUDAH/KALKUDAH : *Hotels*
Imperial Oceanic 66 A/C A/I (VE)
Passekudah
Tel: 065-7206/7
Contact tel: 36854

Sun & Fun 60 R/O (VE)
National Holiday Resort
Kalkudah
Tel: 237 Valaichenai
Reservations tel: 29804, 81714

Sun Tan Beach 22 R/O B/B (VE)
Passekudah/Kalkudah Bung.
Tel: 065-7321 Valaichenai or
Colombo 27206, 31721

Guest House
Sea Sans A/I (B)
Arugambai, Pottuvil
Tel: 21, Agrapatne

POLONNARUWA : *Hotels*
Amaliyan Nivas 34 A/C R/O B/B (B)
National Holiday Resort
New Town, Polonnaruwa
Tel: 541198 Polonnaruwa

Araliya 30 R/O B/B (B)
National Holiday Resort
Polonnaruwa
Tel: Polonnaurwa 627
Reservations tel: 37420

Hotel Seruwa 40 A/C A/I B/B (M)
National Holiday Resort
Polonnaruwa
Tel: 027-2411/2 Polonnaruwa
Contact tel: 23501/23504

Rest House A/I B/B (M)
Polonnaruwa
Tel: 027-2299 Polonnaruwa
Contact tel: 23504

RATNAPURA : *Hotels*
Ratnaloka Tour Inns 53 A/C F/B R/O (E)
Kosgala, Kahangama
Ratnapura
Tel: 455

SIGIRIYA : *Hotels*
Hotel Sigiriya 32 R/O F/B (M)
Sigiriya
Tel: 066-8311 Dambulla
Contact tel: 32895

Sigiriya Rest House 17 A/I (M)
Sigiriya
Tel: 2 Kibissa, contact tel: 23504

TANGALLA : *Hotels*
Tangalla Bay　　　　　　36 R/O B/B (E)
Pallikudawa, Tangalla
Tel: 0416-246

Guest Houses
Peace Haven Beach Hotel　　12 R/O (M)
Goyambokka, Tangalla　　　　Suite
Contact tel: 95455

TISSAMAHARAMA :
Rest House　　　　　　　37 A/I (M)
Tissamaharama
Tel: 95 Tissamaharama or
Contact tel: 23501, 23504

Guest House
Priyankara　　　　　　　12 A/I (M)
Kataragama Road
Tissamaharama

TRINCOMALEE: *Hotels*
Blue Lagoon　　　　　　40 R/O B/B (B)
Nilaveli
Trincomalee
Tel: 26 Nilaveli
Contact tel: 28650, 35285

Club Oceanic　　　75 A/C R/O A/I (E)
Uppuveli, Trincomalee
Tel: 026-2611
Contact tel: 24916

Moonlight Beach Lodge　　55 Non A/C (E)
Nilaveli, Trincomalee　　　　R/O B/B
Tel: 25984 and 22 and 23 Nilaveli

Nilaveli Beach　　　　　70 A/C R/O (E)
11th Mile Post　　　　　Non A/C R/O
Nilaveli
Tel: 95 Nilaveli

7 Islands Hotels　　　25 A/C R/O B/B (E)
Orr's Hill Road
Tel: 373 Trincomalee

Moonlight Beach Lodge　　55 Non A/C (E)
Nilaveli, Trincomalee　　　　R/O B/B
Tel: 25984 and 22 and 23 Nilaveli

Nilaveli Beach　　　　　70 A/C R/O (E)
11th Mile Post　　　　　Non A/C R/O
Nilaveli
Tel: 95 Nilaveli

WELIGAMA : *Hotels*
Bay Beach　　　　　　　32 R/O B/B (E)
Kapparatota
Weligama
Contact tel: 0415-201

Ruhunu Guest House　　　6 A/I B/B (M)
Mudaliyar
D.M. Samaraweera Mawatha
Weligama
Tel: 0415-228

WILPATTU : *HotelsD*
Hotel Wilpattu　　　　　R/O B/B (B)
Kala Oya Cabanas
Contact tel: 24624

Preshamel Safari　　　12 B/B R/O (B)
Pahalamaragahawewa
Wilpattu
Contact tel: 32469

WIRAWILA : *Hotels*
Sanasuma Holiday Resort　　50 A/I (M)
Wirawila Estate
Wirawila
Contact tel: 597467

Guest Houses
Ibis Safari Lodge　　　　　6 B/B (B)
Wirawila
Contact tel: 82069

YALA : *Hotels*
Browns Safari Beach Hotel
Amaduwa　　　　50 A/I R/O B/B (B)
Yala
Tel: 031-2031

Yala Safari　50 R/O B/B (B)
Beach Hotel
Amaduwa
Yala
Tel: 33145, 28842

Paying Guest Accommodation

ALUTHGAMA
Mrs H.S. de Silva
River View Inn　　　　　　　(B)
Kaluwamodera
Aluthgama

AMBALANGODA
Miss s. Kumudini Akuretiya
Shangrela Beach Inn (B)
Sea Beach Road
Ambalangoda
Tel: 097-342

Mrs Charmaine Fernando
"Brooklyn" (B)
New Galle Road
Ambalangoda
Tel: 097-359

COLOMBO
A. Wayfarers Inn (B)
77 Rosmead Place
Colombo 7
Tel: 93936

Mrs Rohini Abeysekera
2A De Fonseka Road (B)
Off Dickman's Road
Colombo 5
Tel: 87188, 85527

Mrs N. Abeysuriya (B)
80/3 Layarda Road
Colombo 5
Tel: 82567

Mrs P. Ambanpola (B)
9 Skelton Gardens
Havelock Park
Colombo 6

Mrs M.M. Bodinagoda (B)
17 Don Carolis Road
Colombo 5
Tel: 86160

Mrs Verita Bakelman (B)
"La Tranuiller"
26B Relevent Road, Colombo 4
Tel: 89578

Mrs D. Bandara (B)
24 Castle Lane
Bambalapitiya
Tel: 82646

Mrs Benedicta Basnayaka (B)
Villa Benedicta
290 Hendala Wattala
Tel: 530443

Mrs D. Brito (B)
15/1 Alfred House Gardens
Colombo 3
Tel: 86659

Mrs Coomaraswamy (B)
391 Havelock Road
Colombo 5
Tel: 84457

Mrs Nelum Cooray (B)
3A Elibank Road
Colombo 5
Tel: 81064

Mrs L. Chandrasena (B)
46 Harmers Avenue
Colombo 6
Tel: 87119

Mrs R. Dias (B)
170/1 Maya Avenue
Colombo 5
Tel: 589853

Mrs S. Gajendran (B)
155/3 Maya Avenue
Havelock Town
Colombo 6
Tel: 82496

Dr L.R. Dias (B)
14 De Fonseka Road
Colombo 5
Tel: 84363

Mrs B. De Mel (B)
53 Bullers Lane
Colombo 7
Tel: 83146

Mrs Chandra Dissanayake (B)
8, 36th Lane, Off Bullers Lane
Colombo 8
Tel: 95376

Mrs Ratnasiri Fernando (B)
21 Fareed Place
Colombo 4
Tel: 84708

Mrs C.D. Fernando (B)
30/7 Park Road, Colombo 5
Tel: 85319

Mrs J.E. De Fonseka
3/1A De Fonseka Road
Colombo 5
Tel: 84693

Mrs M.I. Gajasinghe
"New Haven"
462/2 Castle Street
Borella
Tel: 98127

Mrs Carmen gunasekera
85 Dharmapala Mawatha
Colombo 7
Tel: 93010

Mrs S. Goonetilleke
29 Spathodea Avenue
Havelock Town
Colombo 5
Tel: 81861

Mrs S. Gunawardena
9 Carwill Place
Colombo 3
Tel: 21813

Mrs C.S. Ilangakoon
97/3 Rosemeed Place
Colombo 7
Tel: 94749

Dr S. Indraratna
7 Esther Avenue
Off Park Road
Colombo 5
Tel: 85869

Mr L.W.P. Jayatillake
36/15 Rosemeed Place
Colombo 7
Tel: 93669

Mrs B/H/S. Jayawardena
"Meenalle"
423 Galle Road
Colombo 3
Tel: 82027

Mrs C.G. Jayawardena
31 Kottawa Road
Mirihana Road
Nugegoda
Tel: 55-2796

(B) Mrs S. Jayawardena
42 Kuruppu Road
Colombo 8
Tel: 93820

(B) Mrs M. Karunaratne
39/3 Gregory's Road
Colombo 7
Tel: 91702, 94146

(B) Mr D.J.V. Kannagara
49 Station Road
Wattala
Tel:530359

Mrs V. Kotalawela
(B) 17 Tournour Road
Colombo 8
Tel: 598521

Mrs M. Loyola
2 Dickman's Path
(B) Colombo 5
Tel: 86885

Mrs P. Manchanayake
6 Mahasen Mawatha
(B) Nawala Road
Nugegoda
Tel: 55334

Dr J.J. Mendis
201/3 Rajagiriya Road
Rajagiriya

Mrs Ranjani Muttuvelu
"Prakash Tour Inn"
60/1 Barnes Places
Colombo 7
Tel: 93389

Mrs P. Nanayakkara
20 Chelsea Gardens
Colombo 3
Tel: 20942

Mrs S.R. Parana-Vithana
100 Kynsey Road
Colombo 8
Tel: 93318

Index